Betty Crocker

cookies

100 Favorite Recipes

WILEY

Wiley Publishing, Inc

Library of Congress Cataloging-in-Publication Data:

Crocker, Betty.
  Betty Crocker cookies : 100 favorite recipes.
    p. cm.
  Includes index.
  ISBN 978-1-4351-2569-8 (cloth : alk. paper)
  1. Cookies. I. Title. II. Title: Cookies.
  TX772.C694 2009
  641.81654 — dc22

                    2008026379

General Mills

Editorial Director:
Jeff Nowak

Publishing Manager:
Christine Gray

Recipe Development and Testing:
Betty Crocker Kitchens

Photography:
General Mills Photography Studios and
Image Library

Wiley Publishing, Inc.

Publisher: Natalie Chapman

Executive Editor: Anne Ficklen

Editor: Adam Kowit

Production Manager: Michael Olivo

Cover Design: Suzanne Sunwoo

Interior Design and Layout: Indianapolis
Composition Services

Photography Art Direction: Tai Blanche

Manufacturing Manager: Tom Hyland

Manufactured in China
10 9 8 7 6 5 4 3 2 1

Cover photo: Extraordinary Chocolate Chip
Cookies (page 14)

Our Betty Crocker Kitchens seal guarantees success in your kitchen. Every recipe has been tested in America's Most Trusted Kitchens™ to meet our high standards of reliability, easy preparation and great taste.

Find more great ideas at *BettyCrocker*.com.

Dear Friends,

Cookies aren't just for special occasions—they are the occasion. Remember baking cookies with Mom or Grandma when you were a kid? The wonderful smell, the spoons to lick, the scrumptious cookies you'd helped make yourself.

Now it's your turn to pass those pleasures on. Let the little ones cut gumdrop shapes for the Jewels and Stars Bars. Pile up a platter with warm-from-the-oven Extraordinary Chocolate Chip Cookies for family night in the great room.

Cookies make great gifts too! Tie a ribbon around a set of Six-Layer Brownies to mail to someone miles away but near in your heart. Or box up a batch of Holiday Lime Cooler Cookies for the cookie exchange just around the corner.

Near or far, young or old, everyone you know will shower you with oohs and aahs for the sensational sweets you share with love.

So grab your favorite mixing bowl and stir up some magic!

Enjoy,

Betty Crocker

contents

Cookies & Brownies & Bars, Oh My!

Who doesn't like homemade cookies, especially when they're just out of the oven? They're fun to eat, easy to tote and guaranteed to please any crowd. To make sure you get the best results every time, here are some easy tips for making and storing them and for making cookie care packages to send through the mail.

Cookie Success Tips

- To make drop cookies uniform in size and shape, use a spring-handled cookie scoop. Look for scoops at the grocery store or kitchen specialty shops. Select the size of the scoop based on how large or small you like your cookies.

- Have three or four cookie sheets on hand, so as you bake one sheet you can get another one ready to go.

- Use cookie sheets that are at least two inches narrower and shorter than the inside dimensions of your oven, so heat circulates around them.

- Shiny aluminum cookie sheets (both smooth and textured) give best results for evenly baked and browned cookies.

- It's best to bake only one cookie sheet at a time, using the middle oven rack. If you want to bake two sheets at once, put one on the oven rack in the upper third of the oven and one on the oven rack in the lower third. Switch their positions halfway through the baking time.

- Check cookies at the minimum bake time. Even one minute can make a difference with cookies, especially those high in sugar and fat. The longer cookies bake, the more brown, crisp or hard they become.

- Always put cookie dough on completely cooled cookie sheets. Cookies spread too much if put on a hot, or even a warm, cookie sheet. Cool cookie sheets quickly by popping them in the refrigerator or freezer or by running cold water over them (dry completely and grease again if needed).

Brownie and Bar Success Tips

- For best results, use the pan size and baking time called for in the brownie or bar recipe.

- Shiny aluminum baking pans are best for baking bars, because they reflect heat and prevent bars from overbrowning and becoming hard.

- Line your pan with aluminum foil when making several batches of bars or brownies. Grease only the bottom of the foil. Brownies are easy to lift from the pan and cut on the foil when cool. And your pan is ready to line and bake the next batch!

- Spread or press dough for bars and brownies evenly to the sides of the pan. For dough that is sticky, try one of these methods:
  - Wet your hands or spray them with cooking spray.
  - Place a piece of plastic wrap directly on top of the dough, and smooth out the top of the dough with your hands.
  - Place your hands in plastic bags.

- Be sure to follow your recipe's "doneness test." When a toothpick inserted two inches from the side of the pan comes out clean or almost clean, brownies are ready.

- For easier cutting, cool brownies and bars completely and use a plastic knife.

Preparing Sheets and Pans

Use shortening or cooking spray to grease cookie sheets and baking pans, but only when the recipe specifies greasing. Butter, margarine and vegetable oil aren't recommended for greasing pans and cookie sheets—they can burn and stick to metal surfaces, making cleanup very difficult.

Storing Cookies and Bars

Here's a great tip to remember: Store crisp cookies with other crisp ones; soft cookies with other soft ones; chewy cookies with other chewy ones. Never store crisp and chewy or soft cookies together in the same container or the crisp cookies will become soft.

- Store crisp cookies at room temperature in a loosely covered container.

- Store chewy and soft cookies at room temperature in resealable food-storage plastic bags or tightly covered containers.

- Let frosted or decorated cookies set or harden before storing; store them between layers of waxed paper, plastic wrap or foil.

- Store different flavors of cookies in separate containers, or they will pick up the flavors of the other cookies.

- Most bars can be stored tightly covered, but check the recipe to be sure; some may need to be loosely covered and others need to be refrigerated.

- To freeze cookies and bars, tightly wrap and label; freeze unfrosted cookies up to 12 months and frosted cookies up to three months. Do not freeze meringue, custard-filled or cream-filled cookies. Put delicate frosted or decorated cookies in single layers in freezer containers and cover with waxed paper before adding another layer. Thaw most cookies, covered, in the container at room temperature for one to two hours. For crisp cookies, remove from the container to thaw.

Send Your Cookies with Love

Food gifts are a wonderful way to send your love to those who are miles away but near in your heart.

MAKE 'EM PRETTY

For unique packages or to embellish the packages you're sending:

- Use berry baskets, take-out containers or large coffee mugs as packaging.

- Place smaller cookies or treats in cellophane bags and tie with ribbon; protect them in a firm container.

- Shop for scrapbooking paper, stickers and/or decorations to create a themed package perfect for the recipient.

BROWN PAPER PACKAGES TIED UP WITH . . .

- Wrap cookies in pairs, back to back. Brownies and bars will remain fresher if left uncut; just wrap the whole rectangle or square in plastic wrap or foil. (Include a plastic knife, especially for the college student.)

- Rigid plastic containers, firm-sided cardboard boxes or sturdy metal cans are great for shipping. Before adding treats, line them with plastic wrap or foil.

- Fill each container until almost full, allowing space at the top to cushion with crumpled waxed paper, paper towels or packing peanuts to prevent food from breaking or crumbling; seal container with lid or top.

- Pack filled containers in a firm cardboard box. Cushion with bubble wrap, crumpled paper, shredded paper or packing peanuts.

Super-Easy No-Bake Cookies

On those days when you'd rather not fire up the oven, try these yummy treats.

Goldfish Drops

Prep Time: **10 min**
Start to Finish: **1 hr 10 min**
About 3 dozen cookies

1 cup butterscotch chips
1 tablespoon shortening
1 package (6 oz) original-flavored tiny fish-
    shaped crackers (about 3½ cups)
1 cup broken pretzel sticks

1.   Grease cookie sheet. In 3-quart saucepan, melt butterscotch chips and shortening over low heat, stirring constantly, until smooth; remove from heat. Stir in crackers and pretzels until well coated.

2.   On cookie sheet, drop mixture by rounded tablespoonfuls. Let stand about 1 hour or until firm. Carefully remove from cookie sheet.

> **1 Cookie:** Calories 60 (Calories from Fat 25); Total Fat 3g (Saturated Fat 1g); Cholesterol 0mg; Sodium 65mg; Total Carbohydrate 7g (Dietary Fiber 0g); Protein 1g

Peanut Drops are good, too! Substitute white vanilla baking chips for the butterscotch chips and salted peanuts for the pretzel sticks.

No-Bake Apricot Balls

Prep Time: **15 min**
Start to Finish: **15 min**
About 2 dozen cookies

1 package (6 oz) dried apricots
1 cup hazelnuts
2½ cups graham cracker crumbs
1 can (14 oz) sweetened condensed
    milk (not evaporated)

1.   Place apricots and hazelnuts in food processor. Cover and process, pulsing on and off, until finely chopped. Place mixture in large bowl. Stir in cracker crumbs and condensed milk.

2.   Shape mixture into 1-inch balls. Cover tightly and store in refrigerator up to 2 weeks or freeze up to 2 months.

> **1 Cookie:** Calories 35 (Calories from Fat 10); Total Fat 1g (Saturated Fat 0g); Cholesterol 0mg; Sodium 15mg; Total Carbohydrate 5g (Dietary Fiber 0g); Protein 1g

How about Apple Balls instead? Replace the apricots with dried apples and the hazelnuts with walnuts. Perk up the flavor with a dash of cinnamon.

Peanut Butter–Marshmallow Treats

Prep Time: **5 min**
Start to Finish: **15 min**
36 Squares

32 large marshmallows or 3 cups minia-
    ture marshmallows
¼ cup butter or margarine
½ teaspoon vanilla
5 cups sweetened corn puff cereal with
    peanut butter and cocoa

1.   Spray 9×9-inch pan with cookie spray. In 3-quart saucepan, heat marshmallows and butter over low heat, stirring constantly, until marshmallows are melted and mixture is smooth; remove from heat. Stir in vanilla.

2.   Stir in half of the cereal at a time until evenly coated. Press mixture evenly in pan; cool. Cut into 6 rows by 6 rows.

> **1 Square:** Calories 45 (Calories from Fat 10);
> Fat 1g (Saturated Fat 0g); Cholesterol 0mg;
> Sodium 60mg; Carbohydrate 9g (Dietary
> Fiber 0g); Protein 0g

Just for fun, roll the cereal mixture into balls instead of pressing into the pan. Let the kids help!

Golden Cereal Nut Clusters

Prep Time: **10 min**
Start to Finish: **1 hr 10 min**
About 2 dozen cookies

½ pound vanilla-flavored candy coating
3 cups honey graham cereal
½ cup salted peanuts
½ cup miniature marshmallows

1.   Chop candy coating into small pieces; in heavy 10-inch skillet, place chopped candy coating. Cover and heat over low heat about 5 minutes or until coating is soft; remove from heat. Stir until smooth and creamy.

2.   Stir in cereal until well coated. Stir in peanuts and marshmallows. On waxed paper, drop mixture by rounded tablespoonfuls, or spread mixture evenly on waxed paper or foil. Let stand 1 to 2 hours or until completely set.

> **1 Cookie:** Calories 95 (Calories from
> Fat 45); Total Fat 9g (Saturated Fat 2g);
> Cholesterol 5mg; Sodium 60mg;
> Total Carbohydrate 11g (Dietary Fiber 0g);
> Protein 2g

Oh, Chocolate Cereal-Nut Clusters would taste good! All you need to do is substitute chocolate-flavored candy coating for the vanilla coating.

Extraordinary Chocolate Chip Cookies

Fresh Mint Chocolate Chip Cookies

Mocha-Toffee Chocolate Cookies

Double-Chocolate Cherry Cookies

White Chocolate Chunk Macadamia Cookies

Monster-Style Cookies

Oatmeal-Raisin Cookies

Old-Fashioned Peanut Butter Cookies

Crunchy Muncher Cookies

Peanutty Granola Cookies

Trail Mix Cookies

Spicy Pumpkin Cookies

Cran-Orange 'n Date-Nut Cookies

Orange-Frosted Cranberry Cookies

Apricot Spice Cookies

Malted Madness Cookies

Marvelously Minty Cookies

Super-Easy Macaroon Chewies

1

easy drop cookies

Extraordinary Chocolate Chip Cookies

Prep Time: 1 hr ▪ Start to Finish: 1 hr ▪ About 6 dozen cookies

1½ cups butter or margarine, softened
1¼ cups granulated sugar
1¼ cups packed brown sugar
1 tablespoon vanilla
2 eggs
4 cups all-purpose flour
2 teaspoons baking soda
½ teaspoon salt
1 bag (24 oz) semisweet chocolate chips (4 cups)

1 Heat oven to 350°F. In large bowl, beat butter, granulated sugar, brown sugar, vanilla and eggs with electric mixer on medium speed or mix with spoon, until light and fluffy. Stir in flour, baking soda and salt (dough will be stiff). Stir in chocolate chips.

2 On ungreased cookie sheet, drop dough by tablespoonfuls 2 inches apart; flatten slightly.

3 Bake 11 to 13 minutes or until light brown (centers will be soft). Cool 1 to 2 minutes; remove from cookie sheet to cooling rack.

1 Cookie: Calories 140 (Calories from Fat 60); Total Fat 7g (Saturated Fat 4g); Cholesterol 15mg; Sodium 80mg; Total Carbohydrate 18g (Dietary Fiber 0g); Protein 1g

Making these cookies will go a lot faster if you use a cookie/ice-cream scoop. Level off the cookie dough in the scoop on the edge of the bowl.

Fresh Mint Chocolate Chip Cookies

Prep Time: 30 min ■ Start to Finish: 30 min ■ About 3½ dozen cookies

1⅓ cups sugar
¾ cup butter or margarine, softened
1 tablespoon finely chopped fresh mint leaves
1 egg
2 cups all-purpose flour
1 teaspoon baking soda
½ teaspoon salt
1 package (10 oz) mint chocolate chips (1½ cups)

1 Heat oven to 350°F. In large bowl, beat sugar, butter, mint and egg with electric mixer on medium speed, or mix with spoon. Stir in flour, baking soda and salt. Stir in chocolate chips.

2 On ungreased cookie sheet, drop dough by rounded tablespoonfuls about 2 inches apart. Bake 11 to 13 minutes or until golden brown. Cool 1 to 2 minutes; remove from cookie sheet to cooling rack.

1 Cookie: Calories 120 (Calories from Fat 55); Total Fat 6g (Saturated Fat 3g); Cholesterol 15mg; Sodium 90mg; Total Carbohydrate 15g (Dietary Fiber 0g); Protein 1g

Try raspberry chocolate chips instead of the mint variety.

Mocha-Toffee Chocolate Cookies

Prep Time: 1 hr 10 min ▪ Start to Finish: 1 hr 10 min ▪ About 5 dozen cookies

4 teaspoons instant espresso powder or instant coffee granules
2 teaspoons vanilla
1 box (1 lb 2.25 oz) butter recipe chocolate cake mix with pudding in the mix
½ cup butter or margarine, softened
2 eggs
1 cup miniature semisweet chocolate chips
½ cup English toffee bits

1 Heat oven to 350°F. In small bowl, stir together coffee and vanilla until coffee is dissolved. In large bowl, mix cake mix, coffee mixture, butter and eggs with spoon until soft dough forms. Stir in chocolate chips and toffee bits.

2 On ungreased cookie sheet, drop dough by rounded teaspoonfuls about 2 inches apart.

3 Bake 7 to 10 minutes or until surface appears dry. Cool 1 minute; remove from cookie sheet to cooling rack.

1 Cookie: Calories 80 (Calories from Fat 35); Total Fat 4g (Saturated Fat 2g); Cholesterol 10mg; Sodium 100mg; Total Carbohydrate 10g (Dietary Fiber 0g); Protein 0g

Who wants coffee? Enjoy a little extra jolt by gently pressing one chocolate-covered coffee bean into the center of each cookie before baking.

Double-Chocolate Cherry Cookies

Prep Time: 1 hr ▪ Start to Finish: 1 hr ▪ About 4 dozen cookies

1¼ cups sugar
1 cup butter or margarine, softened
¼ cup milk
¼ teaspoon almond extract
1 egg
1¾ cups all-purpose flour
⅓ cup unsweetened baking cocoa
½ teaspoon baking soda
1 cup quick-cooking oats
1 cup semisweet chocolate chips
1 cup dried cherries

1 Heat oven to 350°F. In large bowl, beat sugar, butter, milk, almond extract and egg with electric mixer on medium speed until smooth. Stir in remaining ingredients. On ungreased cookie sheet, drop dough by rounded tablespoonfuls about 2 inches apart.

2 Bake 10 to 12 minutes or until almost no indentation remains when touched in center and surface is no longer shiny. Immediately remove from cookie sheet to cooling rack.

1 Cookie: Calories 110 (Calories from Fat 45); Total Fat 5g (Saturated Fat 3g); Cholesterol 15mg; Sodium 45mg; Total Carbohydrate 15g (Dietary Fiber 0g); Protein 1g

White Chocolate Chunk Macadamia Cookies

Prep Time: 1 hr ■ Start to Finish: 1 hr ■ About 2½ dozen cookies

1 cup packed brown sugar
½ cup granulated sugar
½ cup butter or margarine, softened
½ cup shortening
1 teaspoon vanilla
1 egg
2¼ cups all-purpose flour
1 teaspoon baking soda
¼ teaspoon salt
1 package (6 oz) white chocolate baking bars, cut into ¼- to ½-inch chunks
1 jar (3.25 oz) macadamia nuts, coarsely chopped

1 Heat oven to 350°F. In large bowl, beat sugars, butter, shortening, vanilla and egg with electric mixer on medium speed until light and fluffy, or mix with spoon. Stir in flour, baking soda and salt (dough will be stiff). Stir in baking bar chunks and nuts.

2 On ungreased cookie sheet, drop dough by rounded tablespoonfuls about 2 inches apart.

3 Bake 11 to 13 minutes or until light brown. Cool 1 to 2 minutes; remove from cookie sheet to cooling rack.

1 Cookie: Calories 190 (Calories from Fat 100); Total Fat 11g (Saturated Fat 4g); Cholesterol 15mg; Sodium 100mg; Total Carbohydrate 21g (Dietary Fiber 0g); Protein 2g

No macadamia nuts on hand? Use walnuts or pecans instead.

Monster-Style Cookies

Prep Time: 45 min ▪ Start to Finish: 45 min ▪ About 1½ dozen cookies

¾ cup creamy peanut butter
½ cup butter or margarine, softened
¾ cup packed brown sugar
½ cup granulated sugar
1 teaspoon vanilla
2 eggs
1¼ cups all-purpose flour
1 teaspoon baking soda
2½ cups quick-cooking or old-fashioned oats
½ cup white vanilla baking chips
½ cup sweetened dried cranberries

1 Heat oven to 375°F. In large bowl, beat peanut butter and butter with electric mixer on medium speed until creamy. Add brown and granulated sugars; beat until fluffy. Beat in vanilla and eggs until well mixed. On low speed, beat in flour and baking soda. Stir in oats, baking chips and cranberries.

2 On ungreased cookie sheet, drop dough by ¼ cupfuls 3 inches apart.

3 Bake 11 to 15 minutes or until edges are golden brown. Cool 1 minute; remove from cookie sheet to cooling rack.

1 Cookie: Calories 300 (Calories from Fat 120); Total Fat 14g (Saturated Fat 6g); Cholesterol 35mg; Sodium 180mg; Total Carbohydrate 38g (Dietary Fiber 2g); Protein 7g

Good things come in small packages too! To make 3½ dozen smaller cookies, drop dough by tablespoonfuls instead of ¼ cupfuls. Bake 8 to 10 minutes.

Oatmeal-Raisin Cookies

Prep Time: 40 min ∎ Start to Finish: 40 min ∎ About 3 dozen cookies

⅔ cup granulated sugar

⅔ cup packed brown sugar

½ cup butter or margarine, softened

½ cup shortening

1 teaspoon baking soda

1 teaspoon ground cinnamon

1 teaspoon vanilla

½ teaspoon baking powder

½ teaspoon salt

2 eggs

3 cups quick-cooking or old-fashioned oats

1 cup all-purpose flour

1 cup raisins, chopped nuts or semisweet chocolate chips, if desired

1 Heat oven to 375°F. In large bowl, beat all ingredients except oats, flour and raisins with electric mixer on medium speed, or mix with spoon. Stir in oats, flour and raisins.

2 On ungreased cookie sheet, drop dough by rounded tablespoonfuls about 2 inches apart.

3 Bake 9 to 11 minutes or until light brown. Immediately remove from cookie sheet to cooling rack.

1 Cookie: Calories 120 (Calories from Fat 60); Total Fat 6g (Saturated Fat 3g); Cholesterol 20mg; Sodium 100mg; Total Carbohydrate 15g (Dietary Fiber 0g); Protein 2g

Quick-cooking and old-fashioned rolled oats are interchangeable unless recipes call for a specific type. Instant oatmeal products are not the same as quick-cooking or old-fashioned oats and should not be used for baking—you will get gummy or mushy results.

Old-Fashioned Peanut Butter Cookies

Prep Time: 1 hr 15 min ▪ Start to Finish: 1 hr 15 min ▪ About 4½ dozen cookies

1 box (1 lb 2.25 oz) yellow cake mix with pudding in the mix
⅓ cup water
1 cup creamy peanut butter
2 eggs
Sugar

1 Heat oven to 375°F. In large bowl, beat half of the cake mix (dry), the water, peanut butter and eggs with electric mixer on medium speed until smooth, or mix with spoon. Stir in remaining cake mix.

2 On ungreased cookie sheet, drop dough by rounded teaspoonfuls about 2 inches apart. Flatten in crisscross pattern with fork dipped in sugar.

3 Bake 10 to 12 minutes or until golden brown. Cool 1 minute; remove from cookie sheet to cooling rack.

1 Cookie: Calories 70 (Calories from Fat 25); Total Fat 3g (Saturated Fat 1g); Cholesterol 10mg; Sodium 85mg; Total Carbohydrate 9g (Dietary Fiber 0g); Protein 2g

How about a sandwich? Cookie, that is. Make Chocolate Peanut Butter Sandwich Cookies by spreading 1 to 2 teaspoons chocolate frosting between bottoms of pairs of cookies.

Crunchy Muncher Cookies

Prep Time: 2 hr 10 min ▪ Start to Finish: 2 hr 10 min ▪ About 9 dozen cookies

1 cup granulated sugar

1 cup packed brown sugar

1 cup butter or margarine, softened

⅔ cup vegetable oil

1 teaspoon vanilla

3 eggs

3½ cups all-purpose flour

1 teaspoon baking soda

1 teaspoon cream of tartar

¼ teaspoon salt

2⅔ cups small pretzel twists, coarsely crushed

1 cup old-fashioned or quick-cooking oats

1 cup Wheaties® cereal or Country® Corn Flakes cereal, slightly crushed

1 cup miniature semisweet chocolate chips

1 cup butterscotch chips

1 Heat oven to 350°F. In large bowl, beat sugars, butter, oil, vanilla and eggs with electric mixer on medium speed until light and fluffy, or mix with spoon. Stir in flour, baking soda, cream of tartar and salt. Stir in remaining ingredients.

2 On ungreased cookie sheet, drop dough by heaping teaspoonfuls about 2 inches apart.

3 Bake 9 to 11 minutes or until light brown. Cool 1 minute; remove from cookie sheet to cooling rack.

1 Cookie: Calories 80 (Calories from Fat 40); Total Fat 5g (Saturated Fat 2g); Cholesterol 10mg; Sodium 60mg; Total Carbohydrate 11g (Dietary Fiber 0g); Protein 0g

Have fun with flavor! Try all chocolate or all butterscotch, or add some peanut butter or white baking chips.

Peanutty Granola Cookies

Prep Time: 1 hr ▮ Start to Finish: 1 hr 45 min ▮ 32 cookies

1 box (1 lb 2.25 oz) butter recipe yellow cake mix with pudding in the mix
½ cup butter or margarine, softened
2 eggs
4 sweet and salty peanut granola bars (from 7.4-oz box), coarsely chopped
½ cup peanut butter chips (from 10-oz bag)
1½ teaspoons shortening

1 Heat oven to 350°F. In large bowl, beat cake mix, butter and eggs with electric mixer on medium speed until smooth. Stir in chopped granola bars. On ungreased cookie sheet, drop mixture by rounded tablespoonfuls about 2 inches apart.

2 Bake 10 to 12 minutes or until set and light golden brown around edges. Let cool on cookie sheet on wire rack 2 minutes. Remove from cookie sheet to cooling rack. Cool completely, about 30 minutes.

3 In microwavable resealable food-storage plastic bag, place peanut butter chips and shortening; seal bag. Microwave on High 15 seconds; squeeze bag. Microwave 15 to 25 seconds longer or until melted; squeeze bag until mixture is smooth. Cut off tiny corner of bag; squeeze bag to drizzle mixture over cookies. Let stand about 10 minutes or until drizzle is set. Store in airtight container.

1 Cookie: Calories 120 (Calories from Fat 50); Total Fat 6g (Saturated Fat 3g); Cholesterol 20mg; Sodium 150mg; Total Carbohydrate 16g (Dietary Fiber 0g); Protein 1g

If you like the flavor combination of peanuts and chocolate, substitute chocolate chips for the peanut butter chips.

Trail Mix Cookies

Prep Time: 1 hr 10 min ■ Start to Finish: 1 hr 10 min ■ About 5 dozen cookies

1 cup granulated sugar
1 cup packed brown sugar
1 cup peanut butter
½ cup butter or margarine, softened
½ cup shortening
2 teaspoons vanilla
2 eggs
2 cups all-purpose flour
1½ cups old-fashioned or quick-cooking oats
1 teaspoon baking powder
1 teaspoon baking soda
2 cups candy-coated chocolate candies
1 cup peanuts
¾ cup raisins

1 Heat oven to 375°F. In large bowl, beat sugars, peanut butter, butter, shortening, vanilla and eggs with electric mixer on medium speed until creamy, or mix with spoon. Stir in flour, oats, baking powder and baking soda thoroughly. Stir in candies, peanuts and raisins.

2 On ungreased cookie sheet, drop dough by rounded tablespoonfuls about 2 inches apart; flatten slightly with fork.

3 Bake 9 to 10 minutes or until light brown. Cool 1 minute; remove from cookie sheet to cooling rack.

1 Cookie: Calories 160 (Calories from Fat 80); Total Fat 8g (Saturated Fat 3g); Cholesterol 10mg; Sodium 80mg; Total Carbohydrate 19g (Dietary Fiber 1g); Protein 3g

Tailor these cookies to suit your taste. It's okay, for example, to omit the peanuts and increase the raisins or substitute walnuts for the peanuts.

Spicy Pumpkin Cookies

Prep Time: 25 min ▪ Start to Finish: 55 min ▪ About 2½ dozen cookies

1 box (1 lb 2.25 oz) yellow cake mix with pudding in the mix
2 teaspoons pumpkin pie spice
1 cup canned pumpkin (not pumpkin pie mix)
¼ cup butter or margarine, softened
½ cup raisins, if desired
1 cup vanilla creamy ready-to-spread frosting (from 1 lb container)

1 Heat oven to 375°F. Lightly grease cookie sheet with shortening. In large bowl, mix cake mix (dry) and pumpkin pie spice. Stir in pumpkin and butter until well blended. Stir in raisins.

2 On cookie sheet, drop dough by generous tablespoonfuls about 2 inches apart.

3 Bake 11 to 12 minutes or until set and light golden brown around edges. Cool 1 to 2 minutes; remove from cookie sheet to cooling rack. Cool completely, about 30 minutes. Spread frosting evenly over cookies.

1 Cookie: Calories 125 (Calories from Fat 35); Total Fat 4g (Saturated Fat 2g); Cholesterol 5mg; Sodium 120mg; Total Carbohydrate 22g (Dietary Fiber 0g); Protein 0g

Treat your taste buds to these spicy, soft cookies along with a glass of cold milk or a cup of hot cider. Sprinkle the tops of the frosted cookies with pumpkin pie spice or ground nutmeg for an extra flavor boost and a special look.

Cran-Orange 'n Date-Nut Cookies

Prep Time: 1 hr ▪ Start to Finish: 1 hr ▪ About 3½ dozen cookies

⅓ cup dried cranberries
¼ cup chopped orange slice candy
¼ cup coarsely chopped pitted dates
2 tablespoons fresh orange juice
1 pouch (1 lb 1.5 oz) sugar cookie mix
2 tablespoons all-purpose flour
½ teaspoon ground cinnamon
¼ teaspoon ground ginger
⅓ cup butter or margarine, melted
1 teaspoon grated orange peel
1 egg
1 cup chopped pistachio nuts
½ cup flaked coconut

1 Heat oven to 375°F. In small bowl, mix cranberries, candy, dates and orange juice; set aside.

2 In large bowl, stir cookie mix, flour, cinnamon and ginger. Stir in melted butter, orange peel and egg until soft dough forms. Stir in cranberry mixture, pistachio nuts and coconut until thoroughly mixed.

3 On ungreased cookie sheet, drop dough by rounded teaspoonfuls about 2 inches apart.

4 Bake 10 to 12 minutes or until edges are light golden brown. Cool 5 minutes; remove from cookie sheet to cooling rack. Store tightly covered.

1 Cookie: Calories 100 (Calories from Fat 40); Total Fat 5g (Saturated Fat 2g); Cholesterol 10mg; Sodium 45mg; Total Carbohydrate 15g (Dietary Fiber 0g); Protein 1g

Orange-Frosted Cranberry Cookies

Prep Time: 1 hr 20 min ∎ Start to Finish: 1 hr 50 min ∎ About 4 dozen cookies

Cookies

1 cup granulated sugar

½ cup packed brown sugar

1 cup butter or margarine, softened

1 teaspoon grated orange peel

2 tablespoons orange juice

1 egg

2½ cups all-purpose flour

½ teaspoon baking soda

½ teaspoon salt

2 cups coarsely chopped fresh or frozen cranberries

½ cup chopped nuts, if desired

Orange Frosting

1½ cups powdered sugar

½ teaspoon grated orange peel

2 to 3 tablespoons orange juice

1 Heat oven to 375°F. Spray cookie sheet with cooking spray.

2 In large bowl, beat sugars, butter, orange peel, orange juice and egg with electric mixer on medium speed, or mix with spoon. Stir in flour, baking soda and salt. Stir in cranberries and nuts. On cookie sheet, drop dough by rounded tablespoonfuls about 2 inches apart.

3 Bake 12 to 14 minutes or until edges and bottoms of cookies are light golden brown. Remove from cookie sheet to cooling rack. Cool completely, about 30 minutes.

4 In small bowl, stir all frosting ingredients until smooth and spreadable. Frost cookies.

1 Cookie: Calories 100 (Calories from Fat 35); Total Fat 4g (Saturated Fat 2g); Cholesterol 15mg; Sodium 65mg; Total Carbohydrate 16g (Dietary Fiber 0g); Protein 0g

Save time and lower the calories! Skip the frosting, and dust cookies and serving plate with powdered sugar.

Apricot Spice Cookies

Prep Time: 1 hr 20 min ▪ Start to Finish: 1 hr 20 min ▪ About 6 dozen cookies

⅔ cup granulated sugar
⅔ cup packed brown sugar
½ cup butter or margarine, softened
½ cup shortening
1 teaspoon baking soda
1 teaspoon ground cinnamon or cardamom
1 teaspoon vanilla
½ teaspoon baking powder
½ teaspoon salt
2 eggs
3 cups quick-cooking oats
1 cup all-purpose flour
¾ cup chopped dried apricots
½ cup finely chopped pecans

1 Heat oven to 375°F. In large bowl, beat all ingredients except oats, flour, apricots and pecans with electric mixer on medium speed until creamy, or mix with spoon. Stir in remaining ingredients.

2 On ungreased cookie sheet, drop dough by rounded teaspoonfuls about 2 inches apart.

3 Bake 8 to 10 minutes or until edges are brown and centers are soft. Cool 1 to 2 minutes; remove from cookie sheet to cooling rack.

1 Cookie: Calories 70 (Calories from Fat 35); Total Fat 4g (Saturated Fat 1g); Cholesterol 10mg; Sodium 50mg; Total Carbohydrate 8g (Dietary Fiber 0g); Protein 1g

For same-size cookies every time, use a spring-handled cookie scoop. You can find them in a variety of sizes at most grocery and discount stores.

Malted Madness Cookies

Prep Time: 45 min ▪ Start to Finish: 1 hr ▪ About 2 dozen cookies

Cookies

1 cup packed brown sugar
½ cup butter or margarine, softened
2 eggs
2 cups all-purpose flour
½ cup chocolate-flavor malted milk
    powder
1 teaspoon baking powder
½ teaspoon baking soda
¼ teaspoon salt

Glaze

1½ cups powdered sugar
¼ cup chocolate-flavor malted milk
    powder
2 to 3 tablespoons milk
½ teaspoon vanilla
1 cup chocolate-covered malted
    milk balls, crushed

1 Heat oven to 350°F. Grease cookie sheet with shortening or cooking spray. In large bowl, beat brown sugar, butter and eggs with electric mixer on medium speed, or mix with spoon, until well blended. Stir in flour, ½ cup malted milk powder, the baking powder, baking soda and salt.

2 On cookie sheet, drop dough by rounded tablespoonfuls about 2 inches apart.

3 Bake 12 to 15 minutes or until edges are set. Cool 1 minute; remove from cookie sheet to cooling rack. Cool completely, about 15 minutes.

4 In medium bowl, mix all glaze ingredients except crushed milk balls with spoon until smooth and spreadable. Spread glaze over cookies. Sprinkle with crushed candies.

1 Cookie: Calories 120 (Calories from Fat 30); Total Fat 4g (Saturated Fat 1g); Cholesterol 15mg; Sodium 110mg; Total Carbohydrate 21g (Dietary Fiber 0g); Protein 1g

Need to plan ahead? Unbaked cookie dough can be frozen in an airtight container up to 9 months. Before baking, thaw frozen dough in the fridge at least 8 hours.

Marvelously Minty Cookies

Prep Time: 1 hr 45 min ▮ Start to Finish: 1 hr 45 min ▮ About 8 dozen cookies

2½ cups sugar
1 cup butter or margarine, softened
½ cup shortening
1 teaspoon vanilla
2 eggs
4 cups all-purpose flour
2 teaspoons baking soda
1 teaspoon salt
3 cups pastel-colored mint candy drops

1 Heat oven to 350°F. In large bowl, beat sugar, butter, shortening, vanilla and eggs with electric mixer on medium speed until light and fluffy, or mix with spoon. Stir in flour, baking soda and salt. Stir in mint chips.

2 On ungreased cookie sheet, drop dough by rounded teaspoonfuls about 2 inches apart.

3 Bake 11 to 13 minutes or until light golden brown. Cool 30 seconds; remove from cookie sheet to cooling rack.

1 Cookie: Calories 80 (Calories from Fat 25); Total Fat 3g (Saturated Fat 2g); Cholesterol 10mg; Sodium 65mg; Total Carbohydrate 12g (Dietary Fiber 0g); Protein 1g

Super-Easy Macaroon Chewies

Prep Time: 1 hr 15 min ■ Start to Finish: 3 hr 15 min ■ About 3 dozen cookies

1 pouch (1 lb 1.5 oz) sugar cookie mix
1 bag (14 oz) flaked coconut
¼ cup milk
1 can (14 oz) sweetened condensed milk (not evaporated)
½ cup semisweet chocolate chips
1 teaspoon butter or margarine

1 In large bowl, stir cookie mix and coconut. Stir in milk and condensed milk until well blended. Cover; refrigerate 2 hours.

2 Heat oven to 375°F. Line cookie sheet with cooking parchment paper or use ungreased cookie sheet. On cookie sheet, drop dough by rounded tablespoonfuls about 2 inches apart.

3 Bake 12 to 14 minutes or until edges are light golden brown. Cool 5 minutes; remove from cookie sheet to cooling rack. Cool completely.

4 In small microwavable bowl, microwave chocolate chips and butter on High 1 to 1½ minutes, stirring every 30 seconds, until melted and smooth. Using fork, drizzle chocolate in lines over cookies. Store loosely covered.

1 Cookie: Calories 170 (Calories from Fat 60); Total Fat 7g (Saturated Fat 5g); Cholesterol 0mg; Sodium 75mg; Total Carbohydrate 24g (Dietary Fiber 0g); Protein 2g

Snickerdoodles

Fudge Crinkles

Hazelnut Crinkles

Pecan Crisps

Rich Peanut Butter Cookies

Apricot Butter Cookies

Orange-Spice Drops

German Chocolate Thumbprints

Almond Thumbprint Cookies

Almond Bonbons

Citrus Biscotti

Snappy Ginger Strips

Ginger-Cranberry Shortbread Wedges

Ginger–Brown Sugar Cookies

Pecan Wafers

Rolled Sugar Cookies

Butterscotch Shortbread

Chocolate-Dipped Shortbread Cookies

Malted Milk Cookies

Apple-Date Swirl Cookies

2

shaped and rolled cookies

Snickerdoodles

Prep Time: 1 hr 10 min ▪ Start to Finish: 1 hr 10 min ▪ About 4 dozen cookies

1 box (1 lb 2.25 oz) white cake mix with pudding in the mix
¼ cup vegetable oil
2 eggs
2 tablespoons sugar
1 teaspoon ground cinnamon

1 Heat oven to 350°F. In large bowl, mix cake mix, oil and eggs with spoon until dough forms (some dry mix will remain).

2 Shape dough into 1-inch balls. In small bowl, mix sugar and cinnamon. Roll balls in cinnamon-sugar mixture. On ungreased cookie sheet, place balls about 2 inches apart.

3 Bake 10 to 12 minutes or until set. Remove from cookie sheet to cooling rack.

1 Cookie: Calories 60 (Calories from Fat 20); Total Fat 3g (Saturated Fat 1g); Cholesterol 10mg; Sodium 80mg; Total Carbohydrate 9g (Dietary Fiber 0g); Protein 0g

For Super Snickerdoodles, shape dough into 1½-inch balls and place them 3 inches apart on the cookie sheet; bake 12 to 14 minutes. You'll get about 26 large cookies.

Fudge Crinkles

Prep Time: 1 hr ▓ Start to Finish: 1 hr 30 min ▓ About 2½ dozen cookies

1 box (1 lb 2.25 oz) devil's food cake mix with pudding in the mix
½ cup vegetable oil
2 eggs
1 teaspoon vanilla
⅓ cup powdered sugar

1 Heat oven to 350°F. In large bowl, mix cake mix, oil, eggs and vanilla with spoon until dough forms.

2 Shape dough into 1-inch balls. Roll balls in powdered sugar. On ungreased cookie sheet, place balls about 2 inches apart.

3 Bake 10 to 12 minutes or until set. Cool 1 minute; remove from cookie sheet to cooling rack. Cool completely, about 30 minutes. Store tightly covered.

1 Cookie: Calories 110 (Calories from Fat 45): Total Fat 5g (Saturated Fat 1g); Cholesterol 15mg; Sodium 140mg; Total Carbohydrate 15g (Dietary Fiber 0g); Protein 1g

Double the chocolate! Instead of rolling the cookies in powdered sugar, dip the tops into chocolate candy sprinkles before baking. For extra fun, stir 1 cup mini candy-coated chocolate baking bits into the dough.

Hazelnut Crinkles

Prep Time: 45 min ▮ Start to Finish: 45 min ▮ About 4 dozen cookies

¾ cup granulated sugar
¾ cup hazelnut spread with cocoa (from 13-oz jar)
½ cup butter or margarine, softened
½ teaspoon vanilla
1 egg
1¾ cups all-purpose flour
1 teaspoon baking soda
¼ teaspoon salt
3 tablespoons white decorator sugar crystals or granulated sugar

1 Heat oven to 375°F. In large bowl, beat granulated sugar, hazelnut spread, butter, vanilla and egg with electric mixer on medium speed, or mix with spoon. Stir in flour, baking soda and salt.

2 Shape dough by rounded teaspoonfuls into 1-inch balls. Roll in sugar crystals. On ungreased cookie sheet, place balls about 2 inches apart.

3 Bake 7 to 9 minutes or until puffed and edges are set. Cool on cookie sheet on wire rack 1 minute. Remove from cookie sheet to cooling rack. Cool completely.

1 Cookie: Calories 90 (Calories from Fat 25); Total Fat 3g (Saturated Fat 5g); Cholesterol 10mg; Sodium 55mg; Total Carbohydrate 11g (Dietary Fiber 0g); Protein 5g

Pecan Crisps

Prep Time: 1 hr 30 min ▮ Start to Finish: 1 hr 30 min ▮ About 5 dozen cookies

2 cups packed brown sugar
1 cup butter or margarine, softened
1 teaspoon vanilla
2 eggs
3 cups all-purpose flour
½ teaspoon baking soda
1 cup chopped pecans, toasted*

1 Heat oven to 350°F. In large bowl, beat brown sugar, butter, vanilla and eggs with electric mixer on medium speed, or mix with spoon, until well blended. Stir in flour, baking soda and pecans.

2 Shape dough into 1¼-inch balls. On ungreased cookie sheet, place balls about 2 inches apart.

3 Bake 10 to 14 minutes or until edges are light golden brown. Remove from cookie sheet to cooling rack.

*To toast pecans, bake in a shallow pan at 350°F for 6 to 10 minutes, stirring occasionally, until light brown.

1 Cookie: Calories 90 (Calories from Fat 40); Total Fat 5g (Saturated Fat 2g); Cholesterol 15mg; Sodium 35mg; Total Carbohydrate 12g (Dietary Fiber 0g); Protein 1g

...h Peanut Butter Cookies

Prep Time: 40 min ▪ Start to Finish: 40 min ▪ About 2 dozen cookies

1 cup packed brown sugar
½ cup peanut butter
½ cup butter or margarine, softened
1 egg
1¼ cups all-purpose flour
¾ teaspoon baking soda
½ teaspoon baking powder
¼ teaspoon salt
1 cup peanut butter chips
Granulated sugar

1 Heat oven to 375°F. In large bowl, beat brown sugar, peanut butter, butter and egg with electric mixer on medium speed until creamy, or mix with spoon. Stir in flour, baking soda, baking powder and salt. Stir in peanut butter chips.

2 Shape dough into 1½-inch balls. Dip tops of balls into granulated sugar. On ungreased cookie sheet, place balls, sugared sides up, about 3 inches apart (do not flatten).

3 Bake 9 to 10 minutes or until light brown. Cool 5 minutes; remove from cookie sheet to cooling rack.

1 Cookie: Calories 170 (Calories from Fat 80); Total Fat 9g (Saturated Fat 3g); Cholesterol 20mg; Sodium 150mg; Total Carbohydrate 19g (Dietary Fiber 0g); Protein 3g

Why not try semisweet or milk chocolate chips instead of the peanut butter chips?

Apricot Butter Cookies

Prep Time: 1 hr 20 min ▮ Start to Finish: 1 hr 50 min ▮ About 4 dozen cookies

Cookies
1 cup butter or margarine, softened
¾ cup powdered sugar
1 teaspoon vanilla
1½ cups all-purpose flour
¼ cup finely chopped dried apricots

Frosting and Garnish
¼ cup butter or margarine, softened
¼ cup apricot preserves
1 cup powdered sugar
3 medium dried apricots, cut into 48 strips

1 Heat oven to 350°F. In medium bowl, beat 1 cup butter, ¾ cup powdered sugar and the vanilla with electric mixer on medium speed until smooth. Beat in flour until well blended. Stir in finely chopped apricots.

2 Shape dough into 1-inch balls. On ungreased cookie sheet, place balls about 2 inches apart.

3 Bake 8 to 12 minutes or until bottoms are light golden brown. Cool 1 minute; remove from cookie sheet to cooling rack. Cool completely, about 30 minutes.

4 In small bowl, beat ¼ cup butter and the apricot preserves with electric mixer on medium speed until smooth. Beat in 1 cup powdered sugar until well blended. Spread frosting over cookies. Top each cookie with apricot strip.

1 Cookie: Calories 80 (Calories from Fat 45); Total Fat 5g (Saturated Fat 3g); Cholesterol 15mg; Sodium 35mg; Total Carbohydrate 9g (Dietary Fiber 0g); Protein 0g

Use kitchen scissors to make quick work of cutting the apricots.

Orange-Spice Drops

Prep Time: 1 hr 5 min ■ Start to Finish: 2 hr 5 min ■ About 3 dozen cookies

1 pouch (1 lb 1.5 oz) sugar cookie mix
⅓ cup mascarpone cheese or 1 package (3 oz) cream cheese
¼ cup butter or margarine, softened
1 tablespoon grated orange peel
1 tablespoon fresh orange juice
¼ teaspoon pumpkin pie spice
1 egg
1 cup finely chopped pecans
2 cups white candy melts, coating wafers or white vanilla baking chips (12 oz)
Edible orange glitter, if desired

1 Heat oven to 375°F. In large bowl, beat cookie mix, mascarpone cheese and butter on low speed until well mixed. Add orange peel, orange juice, pumpkin pie spice and egg; beat until thoroughly mixed.

2 Using small cookie scoop, shape dough into 1-inch balls. Roll balls in pecans. On ungreased cookie sheet, place balls about 2 inches apart.

3 Bake 11 to 13 minutes or until edges are light golden brown. Cool 5 minutes. Remove from cookie sheet to cooling rack. Cool completely.

4 In small microwavable bowl, microwave candy melts uncovered on High 1 to 2 minutes, stirring every 30 seconds, until melted and smooth. Dip each cookie halfway into melted candy, letting excess drip off. Place on waxed paper; let stand until almost set. Sprinkle dipped half of each cookie with edible glitter. Let cookies stand until candy coating is completely set, about 1 hour. Store between sheets of waxed paper in tightly covered container.

1 Cookie: Calories 150 (Calories from Fat 70); Total Fat 8g (Saturated Fat 4g); Cholesterol 10mg; Sodium 65mg; Total Carbohydrate 18g (Dietary Fiber 0g); Protein 2g

Look for edible glitter in the baking section of craft stores or specialty kitchen stores.

German Chocolate Thumbprints

Prep Time: 1 hr 15 min ▮ Start to Finish: 1 hr 30 min ▮ About 3½ dozen cookies

1 box (1 lb 2.25 oz) German chocolate cake mix with pudding in the mix
⅔ cup flaked coconut
¼ cup vegetable oil
2 eggs
⅓ cup coconut pecan creamy ready-to-spread frosting (from 1-lb container)
¼ cup flaked coconut, toasted*

1 Heat oven to 350°F. In large bowl, mix cake mix, ⅔ cup coconut, the oil and eggs with spoon until dough forms.

2 Shape dough into 1-inch balls. On ungreased cookie sheet, place balls about 2 inches apart. Press thumb into center of each cookie to make indentation, but do not press all the way to the cookie sheet. Fill each indentation with level ¼ measuring teaspoon of the frosting.

3 Bake 8 to 11 minutes or until set. Cool 1 minute; remove from cookie sheet to cooling rack. Sprinkle each with ¼ teaspoon of the toasted coconut. Cool completely, about 15 minutes.

*To toast the coconut, bake in a shallow pan at 350°F for 5 to 7 minutes, stirring occasionally, until golden brown.

1 Cookie: Calories 90 (Calories from Fat 35); Total Fat 4g (Saturated Fat 2g); Cholesterol 15mg; Sodium 120mg; Total Carbohydrate 12g (Dietary Fiber 0g); Protein 1g

Pour tall glasses of ice-cold regular or chocolate milk for dipping these chocolate-coconut treasures.

Almond Thumbprint Cookies

Prep Time: 1 hr ▮ Start to Finish: 1 hr ▮ About 3 dozen cookies

¼ cup packed brown sugar
¼ cup shortening
¼ cup butter or margarine, softened
½ teaspoon vanilla
1 egg yolk
1 cup all-purpose flour
¼ teaspoon salt
1 egg white
½ cup finely chopped almonds
About 6 tablespoons strawberry, lemon or lime curd

1 Heat oven to 350°F. In medium bowl, beat brown sugar, shortening, butter, vanilla and egg yolk with electric mixer on medium speed until creamy, or mix with spoon. Stir in flour and salt.

2 Shape dough into ¾-inch balls. Beat egg white slightly with fork. Dip each ball into egg white; roll in almonds. On ungreased cookie sheet, place balls about 1 inch apart. Press thumb into center of each cookie to make indentation, but do not press all the way to the cookie sheet.

3 Bake 10 to 12 minutes or until light brown. Quickly remake indentations with end of wooden spoon if necessary. Immediately remove from cookie sheet to cooling rack. Fill each thumbprint with about ½ teaspoon of the strawberry curd.

1 Cookie: Calories 70 (Calories from Fat 35); Total Fat 4g (Saturated Fat 1g); Cholesterol 10mg; Sodium 30mg; Total Carbohydrate 7g (Dietary Fiber 0g); Protein 1g

Make these cookies even fruitier! Instead of filling the whole batch with strawberry, lemon or lime curd, use a few different flavors of your favorite jam or jelly.

Almond Bonbons

Prep Time: 1 hr 15 min ▪ Start to Finish: 1 hr 45 min ▪ 40 Cookies

Cookies

1½ cups all-purpose flour

⅓ cup powdered sugar

½ cup butter or margarine, softened

3 tablespoons milk

½ teaspoon vanilla

½ package (7 or 8 oz) almond paste
(not marzipan)

Frosting and Decorations

1 cup powdered sugar

½ teaspoon almond extract

4 to 5 tablespoons milk

Edible glitter, white candy sprinkles
or coarse sugar

1 Heat oven to 375°F. In large bowl, beat flour, ⅓ cup powdered sugar, butter, 3 tablespoons milk and the vanilla with electric mixer on medium speed, or mix with spoon until well blended. Cut almond paste into ½-inch slices, and cut each slice into 8 pieces.

2 Shape 1-inch ball of dough around each piece of almond paste. Gently roll to form ball. On ungreased cookie sheet, place balls about 1 inch apart.

3 Bake 10 to 12 minutes or until set and bottoms are golden brown. Remove from cookie sheet to cooling rack. Cool completely, about 30 minutes.

4 In small bowl, mix 1 cup powdered sugar, the almond extract and enough milk for spreading consistency. Dip tops of cookies into frosting. Sprinkle with edible glitter.

1 Cookie: Calories 80 (Calories from Fat 35); Total Fat 4g (Saturated Fat 2g); Cholesterol 5mg; Sodium 15mg; Total Carbohydrate 12g (Dietary Fiber 0g); Protein 1g

Mini paper cupcakes liners or fluted bonbon cups make great holders for these giftable treats.

Citrus Biscotti

Prep Time: 25 min ▮ Start to Finish: 5 hr 40 min ▮ About 2½ dozen biscotti

Biscotti
1 box (1 lb 2.25 oz) lemon cake mix with pudding in the mix
1 tablespoon vegetable oil
2 eggs
2 tablespoons grated lemon peel
1 tablespoon grated lime peel
1 tablespoon grated orange peel

Easy Lemon Glaze
¼ cup lemon creamy ready-to-spread frosting (from 1-lb container)
2 to 4 teaspoons lemon juice

1 Heat oven to 350°F. In large bowl, mix all biscotti ingredients with spoon until dough forms.

2 On large ungreased cookie sheet, shape dough into 14×3-inch rectangle, ½ inch thick. Bake 20 to 25 minutes or until golden brown. Cool on cookie sheet on wire rack 15 minutes.

3 Cut dough crosswise into ½-inch slices. Arrange slices cut side up on cookie sheet. Bake 7 to 8 minutes or until bottoms are light golden brown; turn slices over. Bake 7 to 8 minutes longer or until bottoms are light golden brown. Cool 5 minutes; remove from cookie sheet to cooling rack. Cool completely, about 15 minutes.

4 Mix all glaze ingredients until thin enough to drizzle. Drizzle glaze over tops of biscotti. Let stand about 4 hours or until glaze is set.

1 Biscotti: Calories 100 (Calories from Fat 25); Total Fat 3g (Saturated Fat 1g); Cholesterol 15mg; Sodium 125mg; Total Carbohydrate 16g (Dietary Fiber 0g); Protein 1g

Try them with a cup of a hot citrus-flavored tea—and yes, dunking is allowed!

Snappy Ginger Strips

Prep Time: 40 min ■ Start to Finish: 40 min ■ About 4½ dozen cookies

1 cup sugar
½ cup vegetable oil
¼ cup molasses
1 egg
2 cups all-purpose flour
1½ teaspoons baking soda
½ teaspoon salt
½ teaspoon ground cinnamon
½ teaspoon ground ginger
½ teaspoon ground cloves
4 teaspoons sugar, if desired

1 Heat oven to 375°F. In large bowl, mix 1 cup sugar, the oil, molasses and egg until well blended. Stir in remaining ingredients except 4 teaspoons sugar.

2 Divide dough in half. On ungreased cookie sheet, press half of dough into 14×2-inch strip. Cut strip lengthwise in half; separate strips at least 3 inches. Flatten strips slightly with fork dipped in sugar until ½ inch thick. Sprinkle each strip with 1 teaspoon sugar. Repeat with remaining dough.

3 Bake 6 to 7 minutes or until edges are light golden brown and tops appear cracked; cool 2 minutes. Cut each strip crosswise into 1-inch slices; remove from cookie sheet to cooling rack. Store loosely covered.

1 Cookie: Calories 60 (Calories from Fat 20); Total Fat 2g (Saturated Fat 0g); Cholesterol 0mg; Sodium 60mg; Total Carbohydrate 8g (Dietary Fiber 0g); Protein 0g

Add a little zing to the snap! Drizzle cookies with melted white vanilla baking chocolate (or white baking chips), and sprinkle with chopped crystallized ginger.

Ginger-Cranberry Shortbread Wedges

Prep Time: 30 min ▪ Start to Finish: 40 min ▪ 16 Cookies

⅔ cup butter or margarine, softened
⅓ cup powdered sugar
3 tablespoons finely chopped crystallized ginger
1⅓ cups all-purpose flour
½ cup dried cranberries, chopped
2 teaspoons granulated sugar

1 Heat oven to 350°F. In large bowl, mix butter, powdered sugar and ginger with electric mixer on medium speed, or mix with spoon. Stir in flour and cranberries.

2 On ungreased cookie sheet, pat dough into 9-inch circle. Sprinkle with granulated sugar.

3 Bake about 20 minutes or until golden brown. Cool 10 minutes on cookie sheet on wire rack. Cut into 16 wedges.

1 Cookie: Calories 135 (Calories from Fat 70); Total Fat 8g (Saturated Fat 5g); Cholesterol 20mg; Sodium 60mg; Total Carbohydrate 16g (Dietary Fiber 1g); Protein 1g

Punch up the flavor! Toss ½ cup peanut butter chips, chocolate chips or a combo of both into the dough.

Ginger–Brown Sugar Cookies

Prep Time: 45 min ▪ Start to Finish: 45 min ▪ About 3 dozen cookies

1 cup packed brown sugar
¾ cup butter or margarine, softened
1 teaspoon vanilla
1 egg
2 cups all-purpose flour
½ teaspoon baking soda
½ teaspoon ground ginger
½ cup finely chopped crystallized ginger
2 tablespoons granulated sugar

1 Heat oven to 375°F. In large bowl, beat brown sugar, butter, vanilla and egg with electric mixer on medium speed, or mix with spoon. Stir in flour, baking soda and gingers.

2 Shape dough by rounded teaspoonfuls into 1-inch balls. On ungreased cookie sheet, place balls about 2 inches apart. Flatten to ½-inch thickness with greased bottom of glass dipped in granulated sugar.

3 Bake 8 to 10 minutes or until edges are set. Remove from cookie sheet to cooling rack. Cool completely.

1 Cookie: Calories 95 (Calories from Fat 35); Total Fat 4g (Saturated Fat 2g); Cholesterol 15mg; Sodium 55mg; Total Carbohydrate 14g (Dietary Fiber 0g); Protein 1g

For a frosty white finish, dip half of each cookie in a thin vanilla glaze or melted white chocolate. Let stand on waxed paper until coating sets.

Pecan Wafers

Prep Time: 45 min ▓ Start to Finish: 2 hr 45 min ▓ About 4 dozen cookies

1¾ cups all-purpose flour
¾ cup butter or margarine, softened
¼ cup powdered sugar
¼ cup packed brown sugar
½ teaspoon vanilla
¼ teaspoon baking powder
1 egg
½ cup finely chopped pecans, toasted (see page 42)
48 pecan halves (about ⅔ cup)

1 In large bowl, beat all ingredients except pecans with electric mixer on medium speed until well mixed. Stir in chopped pecans.

2 Place dough on 14-inch length of plastic wrap. Use wrap to shape dough into a log, 12 inches long and 2 inches in diameter. Wrap in plastic wrap and refrigerate at least 2 hours until firm.

3 Heat oven to 375°F. Cut dough into ¼-inch slices with sharp knife. On ungreased cookie sheet, place slices about 1 inch apart. Press 1 pecan half on each cookie.

4 Bake 8 to 10 minutes or until edges begin to brown. Cool 1 minute; remove from cookie sheet to cooling rack.

1 Cookie: Calories 75 (Calories from Fat 45); Total Fat 5g (Saturated Fat 2g); Cholesterol 10mg; Sodium 25mg; Total Carbohydrate 6g (Dietary Fiber 0g); Protein 1g

Tie bundles of cookie stacks with pretty gold ribbon for a simple and tasty gift.

Rolled Sugar Cookies

Prep Time: 1 hr ⬛ Start to Finish: 1 hr ⬛ About 4½ dozen cookies

1 box (1 lb 2.25 oz) white cake mix with pudding in the mix	1 egg
½ cup shortening	Sugar
⅓ cup butter or margarine, softened	1 cup vanilla creamy ready-to-spread frosting (from 1-lb container)
1 teaspoon vanilla, almond or lemon extract	Food colors

1 Heat oven to 375°F. In large bowl, beat half of the cake mix (dry), the shortening, butter, vanilla and egg with electric mixer on medium speed until smooth, or mix with spoon. Stir in remaining cake mix.

2 Divide dough into 4 equal parts. On lightly floured cloth-covered surface and with cloth-covered rolling pin, roll each part ⅛ inch thick. Cut into desired shapes; sprinkle with sugar. On ungreased cookie sheet, place shapes about 2 inches apart.

3 Bake 5 to 7 minutes or until light brown. Cool 1 minute; remove from cookie sheet to cooling rack. In microwavable bowl, microwave frosting uncovered on High 20 to 30 seconds or until melted; stir. Spread frosting evenly over cookies.

Paint colors on freshly iced, glazed or frosted cookies, using a fine-tip brush.

4 Stir together small amounts of water and food color. Paint colors on freshly frosted cookies, using fine-tip brush, then swirl colors with brush or toothpick to create marbled designs. Dry completely before storing.

1 Cookie: Calories 120 (Calories from Fat 55); Total Fat 6g (Saturated Fat 3g); Cholesterol 10mg; Sodium 85mg; Total Carbohydrate 15g (Dietary Fiber 0g); Protein 1g

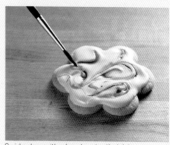

Swirl colors with a brush or toothpick to create marbled designs.

Butterscotch Shortbread

Prep Time: 20 min ▪ Start to Finish: 45 min ▪ About 2 dozen cookies

¼ cup butter or margarine, softened
¼ cup shortening
¼ cup packed brown sugar
2 tablespoons granulated sugar
1 cup plus 2 tablespoons all-purpose flour
¼ teaspoon salt

1 Heat oven to 300°F. In large bowl, beat butter, shortening and sugars with electric mixer on medium speed until creamy, or mix with spoon. Stir in flour and salt. (Dough will be dry and crumbly; use hands to mix completely.)

2 On lightly floured surface, roll dough into 9×6-inch rectangle. Cut into 1½-inch squares. On ungreased cookie sheet, place squares about 1 inch apart.

3 Bake about 25 minutes or until set. Remove from cookie sheet to cooling rack.

1 Cookie: Calories 70 (Calories from Fat 35); Total Fat 4g (Saturated Fat 2g); Cholesterol 5mg; Sodium 65mg; Total Carbohydrate 8g (Dietary Fiber 0g); Protein 1g

Watch the clock when baking these cookies because they brown very little, and the shape does not change.

Chocolate-Dipped Shortbread Cookies

Prep Time: 1 hr ▪ Start to Finish: 1 hr 30 min ▪ About 4 dozen cookies

1 cup butter or margarine, softened
¾ cup powdered sugar
1 teaspoon vanilla
2½ cups all-purpose flour
1 cup semisweet chocolate chips
2 teaspoons shortening

1 Heat oven to 350°F. In large bowl, mix butter, powdered sugar and vanilla until well blended. Stir in flour. (If dough is crumbly, mix in 1 to 2 tablespoons softened butter or margarine.)

2 On lightly floured surface, roll dough ½ inch thick. With sharp knife or cookie cutters, cut small shapes from dough. On ungreased cookie sheet, place shapes about ½ inch apart.

3 Bake 14 to 16 minutes or until set and bottoms are light golden brown. Immediately remove from cookie sheet to cooling rack. Cool completely, about 30 minutes.

4 In small microwavable bowl, place chocolate chips and shortening. Microwave uncovered on High 1 to 1½ minutes, or until melted; stir until smooth. Dip half of each cooled cookie into melted chocolate. Place on waxed paper; let stand until chocolate is set.

1 Cookie: Calories 70 (Calories from Fat 35); Total Fat 4g (Saturated Fat 2g); Cholesterol 10mg; Sodium 25mg; Total Carbohydrate 7g (Dietary Fiber 0g); Protein 0g

Save time and calories! Skip the chocolate dip and enjoy these buttery cookies plain.

Malted Milk Cookies

Prep Time: 1 hr 30 min ▪ Start to Finish: 2 hr ▪ About 5 dozen cookies

Cookies

2 cups packed brown sugar

1 cup butter or margarine, softened

⅓ cup sour cream

2 teaspoons vanilla

2 eggs

4¾ cups all-purpose flour

¾ cup natural-flavor malted milk
powder

2 teaspoons baking powder

½ teaspoon baking soda

½ teaspoon salt

Frosting and Decorations

3 cups powdered sugar

½ cup natural-flavor malted milk
powder

⅓ cup butter or margarine, softened

3 to 4 tablespoons milk

1½ teaspoons vanilla

¾ cup miniature semisweet
chocolate chips, if desired

1 Heat oven to 375°F. In large bowl, beat brown sugar, 1 cup butter, sour cream, 2 teaspoons vanilla and eggs with electric mixer on medium speed until creamy, or mix with spoon. Stir in flour, ¾ cup malted milk powder, baking powder, baking soda and salt.

2 On lightly floured surface, roll one-third of dough at a time ¼ inch thick. Cut into 2½-inch rounds. On ungreased cookie sheet, place rounds about 2 inches apart.

3 Bake 10 to 11 minutes or until almost no indentation remains when touched in center. Immediately remove from cookie sheet to cooling rack. Cool completely, about 30 minutes.

4 Mix all frosting ingredients, except chocolate chips, until smooth and spreadable. Spread frosting on cookies; sprinkle with chocolate chips.

1 Cookie: Calories 115 (Calories from Fat 35); Total Fat 4g (Saturated Fat 2g); Cholesterol 15mg; Sodium 75mg; Total Carbohydrate 19g (Dietary Fiber 0g); Protein 1g

For more chocolaty flavor, use chocolate-flavor malted milk powder instead of the natural-flavor.

Apple-Date Swirl Cookies

Prep Time: 1 hr 20 min ▮ Start to Finish: 3 hr 20 min ▮ About 5 dozen cookies

Filling

1 cup chopped dates

¾ cup finely chopped peeled apple

¼ cup granulated sugar

1 teaspoon grated orange peel

¼ cup orange juice

Cookies

½ cup granulated sugar

½ cup packed brown sugar

½ cup butter or margarine, softened

½ teaspoon vanilla

1 egg

1⅔ cups all-purpose flour

½ teaspoon baking soda

¼ teaspoon salt

¼ teaspoon ground cinnamon

1 In 1-quart saucepan, mix filling ingredients. Cook over medium-high heat, stirring constantly, until mixture boils and thickens. Boil and stir 5 minutes. Cool.

2 In large bowl, beat ½ cup granulated sugar, the brown sugar, butter, vanilla and egg with electric mixer on medium speed, or mix with spoon, until well blended. Stir in flour, baking soda, salt and cinnamon.

3 Between sheets of waxed paper or plastic wrap, roll or pat dough into 16×8-inch rectangle. Remove top paper. Spread cooled filling over dough. Starting with 16-inch side, use waxed paper to lift and roll up dough with filling inside. Wrap tightly. Refrigerate 2 to 3 hours or until firm.

4 Heat oven to 375°F. Cut roll with sharp knife into ¼-inch slices, occasionally cleaning off knife. On ungreased cookie sheet, place slices about 1 inch apart. Bake 8 to 11 minutes or until lightly browned. Remove from cookie sheet to cooling rack.

1 Cookie: Calories 60 (Calories from Fat 15); Total Fat 2g (Saturated Fat 1g); Cholesterol 10mg; Sodium 35mg; Total Carbohydrate 10g (Dietary Fiber 0g); Protein 0g

Shape up your cookies! Rotate the roll slightly with each cut so the roll stays rounded.

3

fun kids' cookies

Polka-Dot Chocolate Drops

Prep Time: 15 min ▪ Start to Finish: 15 min ▪ 2 Dozen cookies

1 cup butterscotch chips
1 cup semisweet chocolate chips
2 cups bran cereal shreds
72 miniature candy-coated chocolate baking bits

1 In 2-quart saucepan, heat butterscotch chips and chocolate chips over low heat, stirring constantly, until melted and smooth.

2 Gently stir in cereal until well coated. On waxed paper, drop mixture by 24 teaspoonfuls. Press 3 baking bits onto each cookie. Refrigerate until firm.

1 Cookie: Calories 100 (Calories from Fat 40); Total Fat 5g (Saturated Fat 3g); Cholesterol 0mg; Sodium 25mg; Total Carbohydrate 14g (Dietary Fiber 3g); Protein 0g

These cute cookies are perfect for letting little hands add the polka dots.

Root Beer Float Cookies

Prep Time: 1 hr 5 min ■ Start to Finish: 1 hr 25 min ■ About 4½ dozen cookies

Cookies

1 cup packed brown sugar

½ cup butter or margarine, softened

2 cups all-purpose flour

⅓ cup finely crushed root beer–
flavored hard candies
(about 10 candies)

1 teaspoon baking powder

½ teaspoon baking soda

¼ teaspoon salt

⅛ teaspoon ground cinnamon

⅛ teaspoon ground allspice

2 eggs

Glaze and Garnish

1 cup powdered sugar

4 to 5 teaspoons root beer or milk

Additional finely crushed root beer–
flavored hard candies,
if desired

1 Heat oven to 350°F. Grease cookie sheet with shortening. In large bowl, beat brown sugar and butter with electric mixer on medium speed until light and fluffy, or mix with spoon. Stir in remaining cookie ingredients.

2 On cookie sheet, drop dough by rounded teaspoonfuls about 2 inches apart.

3 Bake 8 to 10 minutes or until almost no indentation remains when touched in center and edges are golden brown. Cool 1 minute; remove from cookie sheet to cooling rack. Cool completely, about 20 minutes.

4 In small bowl, mix all glaze ingredients except additional candies with spoon until smooth and thin enough to drizzle. Drizzle glaze over cookies. Sprinkle with additional candies.

1 Cookie: Calories 65 (Calories from Fat 20); Total Fat 2g (Saturated Fat 1g); Cholesterol 10mg; Sodium 45mg; Total Carbohydrate 11g (Dietary Fiber 0g); Protein 1g

PB&J Sandwich Cookies

Prep Time: 45 min ▪ Start to Finish: 1 hr 15 min ▪ 18 Sandwich cookies

1 pouch (1 lb 1.5 oz) peanut butter cookie mix
⅓ cup vegetable oil
1 egg
⅓ cup vanilla creamy ready-to-spread frosting (from 1-lb container)
2 tablespoons peanut butter
⅓ cup jam or preserves

1 Heat oven to 375°F. Make and bake cookies as directed on pouch, using oil and egg. Cool completely, about 30 minutes.

2 In small bowl, stir frosting and peanut butter until smooth.

3 For each sandwich cookie, spread generous teaspoon frosting mixture on bottom of 1 cookie; spread scant teaspoon jelly over peanut butter mixture. Top with another cookie, bottom side down.

1 Sandwich Cookie: Calories 200 (Calories from Fat 80); Total Fat 9g (Saturated Fat 2g); Cholesterol 10mg; Sodium 170mg; Total Carbohydrate 28g (Dietary Fiber 0g); Protein 3g

Have cookies ready in a snap! Keep a stash of baked cookies in the freezer ready to be filled and served.

PB&J Strips

Prep Time: 30 min ∎ Start to Finish: 35 min ∎ About 4 dozen cookies

½ cup granulated sugar
½ cup packed brown sugar
½ cup peanut butter
¼ cup shortening
1 egg
1½ cups Original Bisquick® mix
⅓ cup strawberry jam or preserves

1 Heat oven to 375°F. In large bowl, beat sugars, peanut butter, shortening and egg with electric mixer on low speed 30 seconds, scraping bowl constantly. Beat on medium speed 1 minute, scraping bowl occasionally. Stir in Bisquick mix until blended.

2 Place dough on surface sprinkled with Bisquick mix; gently roll in Bisquick mix to coat. Divide dough into 4 parts. Shape each part into roll ¾ inch in diameter and about 13 inches long. On large ungreased cookie sheet, place rolls about 2 inches apart.

3 Make indentation lengthwise in center of each roll with handle of wooden spoon. Spoon jam into resealable food-storage plastic bag; cut off tiny corner of bag. Squeeze bag to pipe preserves evenly into indentations.

4 Bake 9 to 11 minutes until light golden brown and set. Cool on cookie sheet 5 minutes. Cut each roll into 12 slices. Remove from cookie sheet to cooling rack.

1 Cookie: Calories 70 (Calories from Fat 30); Total Fat 3g (Saturated Fat 1g); Cholesterol 0mg; Sodium 80mg; Total Carbohydrate 9g (Dietary Fiber 0g); Protein 1g

For an even sweeter treat, bake the strips without the jam. When strips have cooled, top with chocolate frosting in place of jam.

Bear Cookie Pops

Prep Time: 35 min ▪ Start to Finish: 1 hr 5 min ▪ 12 Cookie pops

1 pouch (1 lb 1.5 oz) peanut butter cookie mix
⅓ cup vegetable oil
1 egg
12 craft sticks (flat wooden sticks with round ends)
24 flat round candies (about ½ inch in diameter)
12 unwrapped milk chocolate candy drops or pieces for baking
1 tube (0.68 oz) red decorating gel

1 Heat oven to 375°F. In medium bowl, stir cookie mix, oil and egg until soft dough forms.

2 Shape dough into 12 balls, using 1½ tablespoons dough for each. On ungreased cookie sheet, place balls about 4 inches apart. Shape remaining dough into 24 balls, using 1 teaspoon dough for each.

3 Insert stick into side of each large ball; place 2 small balls next to each large ball for ears. Press balls evenly until about ¼ inch thick.

4 Bake 11 to 13 minutes or until edges begin to brown. Cool 2 minutes; remove from cookie sheet to cooling rack. Cool completely, about 30 minutes.

5 Add 2 small candies on each cookie for eyes and 1 milk chocolate candy for nose, using gel to attach. Squeeze on gel for mouth.

1 Cookie Pop: Calories 275 (Calories from Fat 115); Total Fat 13g (Saturated Fat 3g); Cholesterol 25mg; Sodium 210mg; Total Carbohydrate 35g (Dietary Fiber 0g); Protein 4g

Send the party home! If you are serving birthday cake at a party, wrap up a couple of cookies for each child as a party gift.

Candy Bar Cookie Pops

Prep Time: 50 min ▪ Start to Finish: 1 hr 20 min ▪ 32 Cookie pops

1 bag (12.5 oz) fun-size milk chocolate–covered candy bars with chewy caramel
    and crispy crunchies, cut in half (32 half-bars)
32 craft sticks (flat wooden sticks with round ends)
1 box (1 lb 2.25 oz) chocolate fudge cake mix with pudding in the mix
½ cup vegetable oil
2 eggs
½ cup colored candy sprinkles or powdered sugar

1 Heat oven to 350°F. Line cookie sheet with foil. Pierce side of each half candy bar with craft stick.

2 In large bowl, beat cake mix, oil and eggs with electric mixer on medium speed until smooth. For each cookie pop, form 1 rounded tablespoonful of dough into a ball; flatten in palm of hand and place candy on top. Form dough around candy, sealing well. Roll in candy sprinkles or powdered sugar to cover completely. On cookie sheet, place cookies about 2 inches apart.

3 Bake 11 to 13 minutes or until set. Cookie will appear moist in the cracks. Cool on cookie sheet 2 minutes. Remove from cookie sheet to cooling rack. Cool completely, about 30 minutes.

1 Cookie Pop: Calories 170 (Calories from Fat 70); Total Fat 8g (Saturated Fat 3g); Cholesterol 15mg; Sodium 150mg; Total Carbohydrate 22g (Dietary Fiber 0g); Protein 2g

These pops are great for a bake sale. Cover each cookie with plastic wrap and tie with colorful curly ribbon.

Pop Art Cookies

Prep Time: 25 min ▪ Start to Finish: 1 hr 5 min ▪ 1 Dozen cookie pops

1 pouch (1 lb 1.5 oz) sugar cookie mix
⅓ cup butter or margarine, melted
2 tablespoons all-purpose flour
1 egg
12 craft sticks (flat wooden sticks with round ends)
1 container (1 lb) creamy ready-to-spread frosting (any white variety)
Food colors in desired colors
Assorted candy decorations

1 Heat oven to 375°F. In medium bowl, stir cookie mix, butter, flour and egg until soft dough forms.

2 On floured surface, roll dough until about ¼ inch thick. Cut with 3-inch round cookie cutter. On ungreased cookie sheet, place shapes about 2 inches apart. Carefully insert a wooden stick into side of each cookie.

3 Bake 9 to 11 minutes or until edges are light golden brown. Cool 1 minute on cookie sheet; remove to cooling rack. Cool completely, about 30 minutes.

4 Divide frosting evenly among 4 small bowls. Tint frosting in 3 of the bowls with different color of food color. Reserve some of the tinted frostings for piping on designs. Frost cookies with remaining white and tinted frostings. For piping, place each tinted frosting in small resealable food-storage plastic bag; cut off tiny corner of bag. Squeeze bag to pipe frostings on cookies in desired designs. Decorate with candy decorations.

1 Cookie Pop: Calories 390 (Calories from Fat 160); Total Fat 18g (Saturated Fat 7g); Cholesterol 30mg; Sodium 230mg; Total Carbohydrate 56g (Dietary Fiber 0g); Protein 2g

Serve cookies from glasses in coordinating colors. Fill the glasses with jelly beans to hold the cookie pops upright.

"Caramel Apple" Cookies

Prep Time: 40 min ▪ Start to Finish: 1 hr 10 min ▪ About 1 dozen cookie pops

½ cup sugar
¼ cup butter or margarine, softened
¼ cup shortening
¾ teaspoon vanilla
1 egg
1½ cups all-purpose flour
¼ teaspoon baking soda
¼ teaspoon salt

1 package (0.13 to 0.14 oz) strawberry, cherry, tropical punch or lemon-lime-flavored unsweetened soft drink mix
About 12 craft sticks (flat wooden sticks with round ends)
24 caramels (from 14-oz bag), unwrapped
2 tablespoons water
Candy sprinkles, if desired

1 Heat oven to 400°F. In large bowl, beat sugar, butter and shortening with electric mixer on medium speed, or mix with spoon. Stir in vanilla and egg. Stir in flour, baking soda, salt and soft drink mix (dry).

2 On lightly floured cloth-covered surface, roll dough ¼ inch thick. Cut with 3-inch round or apple-shaped cookie cutter. On ungreased cookie sheet, place cutouts about 2 inches apart. Carefully insert 1 inch of wooden stick into side of each cookie.

3 Bake 6 to 8 minutes or until edges are light brown. Cool 2 minutes; remove from cookie sheet to cooling rack. Cool completely, about 30 minutes.

4 In 2-quart saucepan, heat caramels and water over low heat, stirring frequently, until melted and smooth. If caramel glaze becomes too stiff, heat over low heat, stirring constantly, until softened.

5 Spread top third of each cookie (opposite wooden stick) with caramel glaze. Hold cookie upright to allow glaze to drizzle down cookie. Sprinkle with candy sprinkles.

1 Cookie Pop: Calories 250 (Calories from Fat 90); Total Fat 10g (Saturated Fat 4g); Cholesterol 30mg; Sodium 170mg; Total Carbohydrate 36g (Dietary Fiber 0g); Protein 3g

Tie colorful ribbons around the sticks to give these treats as gifts.

Quick Candy Cookie Sticks

Prep Time: 40 min ▪ Start to Finish: 40 min ▪ About 56 cookies

½ cup granulated sugar
½ cup packed brown sugar
½ cup vegetable oil
1 teaspoon vanilla
1 egg
1½ cups all-purpose flour
½ teaspoon baking soda
½ teaspoon salt
¾ cup candy-coated chocolate candies

1 Heat oven to 375°F. In large bowl, mix sugars, oil, vanilla and egg with spoon until smooth. Stir in flour, baking soda and salt. Stir in ¼ cup of the candies.

2 Divide dough into fourths. Shape each fourth into roll, about 14 inches long. Place 2 rolls on ungreased cookie sheet. Pat each roll to about ½-inch thickness. Sprinkle 2 tablespoons of the remaining candies on each strip; press lightly.

3 Bake 6 to 8 minutes or until golden brown; cool 2 minutes. Cut each strip crosswise into 1-inch slices; remove from cookie sheet to cooling rack.

1 Cookie: Calories 60 (Calories from Fat 25); Total Fat 3g (Saturated Fat 1g); Cholesterol 0mg; Sodium 35mg; Total Carbohydrate 8g (Dietary Fiber 0g); Protein 0g

Animal Cracker Cookies

Prep Time: 1 hr ■ Start to Finish: 1 hr 30 min ■ About 6 dozen cookies

½ cup shortening
⅓ cup milk
3 tablespoons honey
1 cup whole wheat flour
¾ cup all-purpose flour
½ teaspoon baking powder
¼ teaspoon salt

1 Heat oven to 350°F. In large bowl, beat shortening, milk and honey with electric mixer on medium speed until blended. Stir in remaining ingredients until well blended.

2 Divide dough in half. On lightly floured cloth-covered surface, roll half of dough at a time ⅛ inch thick. Cut with about 1¼- to 1½-inch animal-shaped cookie cutters. On ungreased cookie sheet, place cookies about 1 inch apart.

3 Bake 6 to 8 minutes or until edges are very light brown. Remove from cookie sheet to cooling rack. Cool completely, about 30 minutes.

1 Cookie: Calories 15 (Calories from Fat 10); Total Fat 1g (Saturated Fat 1g); Cholesterol 0mg; Sodium 5mg; Total Carbohydrate 2g (Dietary Fiber 0g); Protein 0g

Just for fun, fill a toy circus-animal train car with bags of cookies.

Paintbrush Cookies

Prep Time: 1 hr 30 min ▮ Start to Finish: 3 hr 30 min ▮ 3½ to 5 Dozen cookies

Cookies

1½ cups powdered sugar
1 cup butter or margarine, softened
1 teaspoon vanilla
½ teaspoon almond extract
1 egg
2½ cups all-purpose flour
1 teaspoon baking soda
1 teaspoon cream of tartar

Egg Yolk Paint

1 egg yolk
¼ teaspoon water
Assorted food colors

1 In large bowl, mix powdered sugar, butter, vanilla, almond extract and egg. Stir in flour, baking soda and cream of tartar. Cover and refrigerate 2 to 3 hours.

2 Heat oven to 375°F. Lightly grease cookie sheet with shortening, or spray with cooking spray. Divide dough in half. On lightly floured surface, roll each half ³⁄₁₆ inch thick. Cut into desired shapes with cookie cutters. On cookie sheet, place cookies about 2 inches apart.

3 In small bowl, mix egg yolk and water. Divide mixture among several small custard cups. Tint each with a different food color to make bright colors. (If paint thickens while standing, stir in a few drops of water.) Paint designs on cookies with small paintbrushes. Bake 7 to 8 minutes or until edges are light brown. Remove from cookie sheet to cooling rack; cool completely.

1 Cookie: Calories 60 (Calories from Fat 30); Total Fat 4g (Saturated Fat 2g); Cholesterol 15mg; Sodium 45mg; Total Carbohydrate 7g (Dietary Fiber 0g); Protein 0g

Kids will have fun mixing the dough, cutting it into shapes and "painting" the cookies. Even if their painting doesn't look the greatest, you'll be pleasantly surprised to see how adorable the baked cookies turn out.

Magic Window Cookies

Prep Time: 1 hr 55 min ■ Start to Finish: 3 hr 25 min ■ About 6 dozen cookies

1 cup sugar
¾ cup butter or margarine, softened
1 teaspoon vanilla
2 eggs
2½ cups all-purpose flour
1 teaspoon baking powder

¼ teaspoon salt
4 rolls (about 1 oz each) ring-shaped
    hard candies or other fruit-
    flavored hard candies

1 In large bowl, beat sugar, butter, vanilla and eggs with electric mixer on medium speed, or mix with spoon. Stir in flour, baking powder and salt. Cover; refrigerate about 1 hour or until firm.

2 Heat oven to 375°F. Cover cookie sheet with cooking parchment paper or foil. On lightly floured cloth-covered surface, roll one-third of dough at a time ⅛ inch thick. Cut into desired shapes. Place on parchment paper. Cut out designs from cookies using smaller cutters or your own patterns. Place whole or partially crushed pieces of candy in cutouts, depending on size and shape of design, mixing colors as desired. Be sure that you use candy pieces that are the same size in the cutouts so it melts evenly. (To crush candy, place in heavy food-storage plastic bag and tap lightly with rolling pin. Because candy melts easily, leave pieces as large as possible.)

3 Bake 7 to 9 minutes or until cookies are very light brown and candy is melted. If candy has not completely spread within cutout design, immediately spread with toothpick or knife. Cool completely on foil, about 30 minutes. Remove cookies gently to cooling rack.

1 Cookie: Calories 50 (Calories from Fat 20); Total Fat 2g (Saturated Fat 1g); Cholesterol 10mg; Sodium 30mg; Total Carbohydrate 8g (Dietary Fiber 0g); Protein 0g

These cookies take a little time to make but are truly works of art! Use candies that are clear or almost clear and not opaque so cookies will look like stained glass windows.

Chex® and O's Snackin' Bars

Prep Time: 15 min ▪ Start to Finish: 45 min ▪ 36 Bars

3 cups Corn Chex® cereal
3 cups Cheerios® cereal
1 package (8 oz) mixed dried fruit
1 cup dried pineapple, chopped
¼ cup butter or margarine
¾ cup packed brown sugar
2 tablespoons all-purpose flour
½ cup light corn syrup

1 Spray 13×9-inch pan with cooking spray. In large heatproof bowl, mix cereals, dried fruit and pineapple.

2 In 2-quart saucepan, melt butter over medium heat. Stir in brown sugar, flour and corn syrup. Heat to boiling, stirring constantly. Boil 1 minute over medium heat, stirring occasionally. Pour over cereal mixture; toss to mix well (mixture will be sticky).

3 Spoon cereal mixture into pan; spread evenly. Cool completely, about 30 minutes, before cutting. For bars, cut into 6 rows by 6 rows.

1 Bar: Calories 90 (Calories from Fat 15); Total Fat 2g (Saturated Fat 1g); Cholesterol 0mg; Sodium 65mg; Total Carbohydrate 19g (Dietary Fiber 1g); Protein 0g

Jewels and Stars Bars

Prep Time: 25 min ■ Start to Finish: 1 hr 55 min ■ 32 Bars

1 bag (10 oz) white vanilla baking chips (1⅔ cups)
½ cup butter or margarine
1¼ cups all-purpose flour
¾ cup sugar
1 teaspoon vanilla
¼ teaspoon salt
3 eggs
1 container (1 lb) vanilla creamy ready-to-spread frosting
Edible glitter, if desired
About ½ cup assorted small gumdrops

1 Heat oven to 350°F. Grease bottom and sides of 13×9-inch pan with shortening; lightly flour.

2 In heavy 2-quart saucepan, heat baking chips and butter over low heat, stirring frequently, just until melted (mixture may appear curdled). Remove from heat; cool. Stir in flour, sugar, vanilla, salt and eggs. Pour batter evenly into pan.

3 Bake 24 to 27 minutes or until toothpick inserted in center comes out clean. Cool completely on cooling rack, about 1 hour.

4 Spread bars with frosting; sprinkle with glitter. Flatten some gumdrops with bottom of glass, and cut with star-shaped cutter. Place gumdrop stars and regular gumdrops (jewels) on frosting. For bars, cut into 8 rows by 4 rows.

1 Bar: Calories 190 (Calories from Fat 80); Total Fat 9g (Saturated Fat 5g); Cholesterol 30mg; Sodium 95mg; Total Carbohydrate 25g (Dietary Fiber 0g); Protein 2g

If gumdrops stick to the glass, grease the bottom of the glass and dip it in sugar before flattening them.

Extreme Bars

Prep Time: 10 min ▪ Start to Finish: 1 hr 30 min ▪ 25 Bars

2 cups Original Bisquick mix
1 cup powdered sugar
½ cup butter or margarine, softened
1 egg
1 package (about 0.13 oz) strawberry-, lemon-, orange- or lime-flavored
     unsweetened soft drink mix
1 cup vanilla creamy ready-to-spread frosting (from 1-lb container)
Candy sprinkles, fruit-flavored gummy ring-shaped candies, gumdrops or jelly
     beans, if desired

1 Heat oven to 350°F. In medium bowl, stir Bisquick mix, powdered sugar, butter, egg and drink mix (dry) until dough forms. On bottom of ungreased 8-inch square pan, pat mixture firmly and evenly.

2 Bake 14 to 18 minutes or until lightly browned around edges. Cool in pan on cooling rack about 1 hour.

3 Spread bars evenly with frosting; sprinkle with candies. For bars, cut into 5 rows by 5 rows.

1 Bar: Calories 150 (Calories from Fat 60); Total Fat 7g (Saturated Fat 4g); Cholesterol 20mg; Sodium 170mg; Total Carbohydrate 20g (Dietary Fiber 0g); Protein 0g

Get in the spirit! Choose a drink mix color to match your kids' school or favorite sports team colors for a team party.

Warm Toasted Marshmallow S'more Bars

Prep Time: 20 min ▪ Start to Finish: 55 min ▪ 24 Bars

1 pouch (1 lb 1.5 oz) sugar cookie mix
1 cup graham cracker crumbs
1 cup butter or margarine, melted
3 cups milk chocolate chips (18 oz)
4½ cups miniature marshmallows

1 Heat oven to 375°F. In large bowl, mix cookie mix and cracker crumbs. Stir in melted butter until soft dough forms. In ungreased 13×9-inch pan, press dough evenly. Bake 18 to 20 minutes or until set.

2 Immediately sprinkle chocolate chips over crust. Let stand 3 to 5 minutes or until chocolate begins to melt. Spread chocolate evenly over crust.

3 Set oven control to broil. Sprinkle marshmallows over melted chocolate. Broil with top 4 to 5 inches from heat 20 to 30 seconds or until marshmallows are toasted. (Watch closely—marshmallows will brown quickly.) Cool 10 minutes. For bars, cut into 6 rows by 4 rows. Serve warm. Store tightly covered.

1 Bar: Calories 310 (Calories from Fat 150); Total Fat 16g (Saturated Fat 8g); Cholesterol 25mg; Sodium 150mg; Total Carbohydrate 39g (Dietary Fiber 0g); Protein 3g

Need a warm-up? To reheat, place individual bars on a microwavable plate. Microwave uncovered on High about 15 seconds or until warm.

4

holiday cookies

Chocolate-Cherry Pinwheels

Prep Time: 2 hr ▧ Start to Finish: 5 hr 30 min ▧ About 4½ dozen cookies

¾ cup butter or margarine, softened
1 cup sugar
2 eggs
3 cups all-purpose flour
1 teaspoon baking powder
½ teaspoon salt
1½ teaspoons almond extract

¼ cup maraschino cherries, finely chopped and drained on paper towels
3 drops red food color
1 teaspoon vanilla
1 tablespoon milk
¼ cup unsweetened baking cocoa

1 In large bowl, beat butter, sugar and eggs with electric mixer on medium speed until smooth. Beat in flour, baking powder and salt until well blended. Place half of dough in another medium bowl.

2 Beat almond extract, cherries and food color into half of dough. Divide cherry dough in half. Wrap each half of cherry dough in plastic wrap; refrigerate about 45 minutes or until firm.

3 Meanwhile, beat vanilla, milk and cocoa into remaining plain dough. Divide chocolate dough in half. Wrap each half of chocolate dough in plastic wrap; refrigerate about 45 minutes or until firm.

4 Place one part of chocolate dough between 2 sheets of waxed paper; roll into 10×7-inch rectangle. Repeat with one part of cherry dough. Refrigerate both about 30 minutes or until firm. Peel top sheets of waxed paper from both doughs. Turn cherry dough upside down onto chocolate dough; roll up doughs together, starting at long side, into a log. Wrap in plastic wrap; refrigerate 2 hours. Repeat with remaining parts of dough.

5 Heat oven to 350°F. Cut rolls of dough into ¼-inch slices with sharp knife. On ungreased cookie sheet, place slices about 1 inch apart.

6 Bake 8 to 11 minutes or until surface appears dull. Remove from cookie sheet to cooling rack.

1 Cookie: Calories 70 (Calories from Fat 25); Total Fat 3g (Saturated Fat 2g); Cholesterol 15mg; Sodium 50mg; Total Carbohydrate 10g (Dietary Fiber 0g); Protein 1g

Shortbread Hearts

Prep Time: 20 min ▮ Start to Finish: 1 hr 55 min ▮ 2 Hearts (6 to 8 servings each)

1 cup butter or margarine, softened
¾ cup powdered sugar
1 teaspoon almond extract
¼ teaspoon red food color
2 cups all-purpose flour
¼ cup sliced almonds
¼ cup white vanilla baking chips
1 teaspoon shortening
Small candy hearts, if desired

1 Heat oven to 350°F. In medium bowl, beat butter, powdered sugar, almond extract and food color with electric mixer on medium speed 2 minutes. Stir in flour and almonds.

2 Divide dough in half; cover half and set aside. On ungreased cookie sheet, place remaining half of dough; press into heart shape, about ¼ inch thick.

3 Bake 15 to 18 minutes or until edges just begin to brown. Cool on cookie sheet 25 minutes; carefully remove from cookie sheet to serving platter. Repeat with remaining dough.

4 In small microwavable bowl, place baking chips and shortening. Microwave uncovered on Medium-High about 1 minute 30 seconds, stirring every 30 seconds, until chips can be stirred smooth. Drizzle over shortbread. Sprinkle with candy hearts.

1 Serving: Calories 565 (Calories from Fat 335); Total Fat 37g (Saturated Fat 22g); Cholesterol 85mg; Sodium 215mg; Total Carbohydrate 54g (Dietary Fiber 2g); Protein 6g

Bake a batch of kisses. To make shortbread lips, press half of dough into oval shape, about ¼ inch thick, on ungreased cookie sheet. Shape each end to form point. Press center of oval to form lips. For fun, bake several hearts and lips, supply lots of frosting and let the fun begin!

Rainbow Egg Cookies

Prep Time: 50 min ▪ Start to Finish: 1 hr 30 min ▪ 18 Sandwich cookies

1 pouch (1 lb 1.5 oz) sugar cookie mix
½ cup margarine or butter, melted
¼ cup all-purpose flour
1 egg
3 food colors
Sugar, if desired
½ container (1 lb) vanilla whipped ready-to-spread frosting

1 Heat oven to 375°F. In medium bowl, stir cookie mix, margarine, flour and egg until soft dough forms. Divide dough evenly among 3 bowls; tint each dough by stirring in a few drops of desired food color.

2 Shape ⅓ cup of each color of dough into a rope about 5 inches long and 1 inch in diameter. On floured surface, place ropes side by side and a little more than ¼ inch apart; roll until ¼ inch thick. Cut with 2- to 2½-inch egg-shaped cookie cutter so each cookie has 3 colors. Sprinkle with sugar. On ungreased cookie sheet, place cookies about 2 inches apart. Repeat with remaining dough. (When rerolling dough scraps, carefully lay matching colors together.)

3 Bake 7 to 9 minutes or until edges are light golden brown. Cool 1 minute; remove from cookie sheet to cooling rack. Cool completely, about 30 minutes. Spread frosting on bottoms of half the cookies. Top with remaining cookies.

1 Cookie: Calories 245 (Calories from Fat 100); Total Fat 11g (Saturated Fat 7g); Cholesterol 30mg; Sodium 105mg; Total Carbohydrate 36g (Dietary Fiber 0g); Protein 1g

For marbled cookies, mix colors of dough scraps just enough to hold together, being careful not to overmix the colors too much or they won't be distinct.

Red, White and Blue Cookies

Prep Time: 1 hr 15 min ▓ Start to Finish: 2 hr 15 min ▓ About 6 dozen cookies

1 cup granulated sugar
1 cup butter or margarine, softened
½ teaspoon almond extract
1 egg
2¼ cups all-purpose flour
2 tablespoons red colored sugar
2 tablespoons blue colored sugar

1 In large bowl, beat granulated sugar, butter, almond extract and egg with electric mixer on medium speed 2 minutes. Stir in flour.

2 Divide dough in half; cover half and set aside. Place remaining half on plastic wrap; press into 8-inch square. Sprinkle with 1 tablespoon each of the red sugar and blue sugar. Using plastic wrap to lift, roll up dough. Repeat with remaining dough and colored sugars. Refrigerate about 1 hour or until firm.

3 Heat oven to 375°F. Cut rolls into ¼-inch slices. On ungreased cookie sheet, place slices about 2 inches apart.

4 Bake 6 to 8 minutes or until edges begin to brown. Cool 1 minute; remove from cookie sheet to cooling rack.

1 Cookie: Calories 50 (Calories from Fat 25); Total Fat 3g (Saturated Fat 2g); Cholesterol 10mg; Sodium 20mg; Total Carbohydrate 6g (Dietary Fiber 0g); Protein 0g

Candy Corn Cookies

Prep Time: 1 hr ▓ Start to Finish: 2 hr 30 min ▓ About 9½ dozen cookies

1 pouch (1 lb 1.5 oz) sugar cookie mix
⅓ cup butter or margarine, melted
1 egg
Orange paste food color
2 oz semisweet chocolate, melted, cooled

1 Line 8×4-inch loaf pan with waxed paper, extending paper over sides of pan. In medium bowl, stir cookie mix, butter and egg until soft dough forms.

2 On work surface, place ¾ cup dough. Knead desired amount of food color into dough until color is uniform. Press dough evenly in bottom of pan.

3 Divide remaining dough in half. Gently press one half of remaining dough into pan on top of orange dough. On work surface, knead chocolate into remaining dough until color is uniform. Press over plain dough in pan, pressing gently to edge of pan. Refrigerate 1½ to 2 hours or until firm.

4 Heat oven to 375°F. Remove dough from pan. Cut crosswise into ¼-inch-thick slices. Cut each slice into 5 wedges. On ungreased cookie sheet, place wedges about 1 inch apart.

5 Bake 7 to 9 minutes or until cookies are set and edges are very light golden brown. Cool 1 minute; remove from cookie sheet. Cool completely. Store in tightly covered container.

1 Cookie: Calories 25 (Calories from Fat 10); Total Fat 1g (Saturated Fat 1g); Cholesterol 0mg; Sodium 15mg; Total Carbohydrate 4g (Dietary Fiber 0g); Protein 0g

Halloween Brownies

Prep Time: 30 min ■ Start to Finish: 3 hr 10 min ■ 24 Brownies

Brownies

1 box supreme brownie mix with
    pouch of chocolate syrup

Water, oil and eggs called for on
    brownie mix box

Frosting and Decorations

1 container (1 lb) creamy white
    ready-to-spread frosting

Neon green, pink and blue food colors

24 large marshmallows

Miniature candy-coated chocolate
    baking bits

Black decorating gel (from 0.68-oz
    tube)

1 roll chewy fruit snack in 3-foot rolls,
    any red variety

Gummy worms

1 Heat oven to 350°F. Make and bake brownies in 13×9-inch pan as directed on box, using water, oil and eggs. Cool completely, about 2 hours. For brownies, cut into 6 rows by 4 rows.

2 Remove lid and foil cover from container of frosting. Microwave frosting uncovered on High about 20 seconds or until frosting can be stirred smooth. Divide warm frosting evenly among 3 small bowls, 1 for each color.

Spider Brownies: Add 5 drops pink food color and 3 drops blue food color to frosting in 1 bowl; mix well. Top each of 8 brownies with 1 large marshmallow. Tuck gummy worms candies under each marshmallow for legs. Spoon 1 tablespoon purple frosting over each marshmallow to coat. Use orange baking bits for eyes. Use black gel for mouths, centers of eyes and eyebrows.

Boo-Brownies: Top each of 8 brownies with 1 large marshmallow. Spoon 1 tablespoon white frosting over each marshmallow to coat. Use black gel for eyes and mouths.

Franken-Brownies: Add 5 drops green food color to frosting in 1 bowl; mix well. Top each of 8 brownies with 1 large marshmallow. Spoon 1 tablespoon green frosting over each marshmallow to coat. Decorate with green baking bits for eyes and ears. Use black gel for mouths and centers of eyes. Cut fruit snack to use for hair.

1 Brownie: Calories 280 (Calories from Fat 100); Total Fat 11g (Saturated Fat 3g); Cholesterol 20mg; Sodium 150mg; Total Carbohydrate 45g (Dietary Fiber 0g); Protein 2g

Pumpkin-Spice Bars with Cream Cheese Frosting

Prep Time: 20 min ▪ Start to Finish: 2 hr 50 min ▪ 49 Bars

Bars

4 eggs

2 cups granulated sugar

1 cup vegetable oil

1 can (15 oz) pumpkin (not pumpkin pie mix)

2 cups all-purpose flour

2 teaspoons baking powder

1 teaspoon baking soda

½ teaspoon salt

2 teaspoons ground cinnamon

½ teaspoon ground ginger

¼ teaspoon ground cloves

1 cup raisins, if desired

Cream Cheese Frosting

1 package (8 oz) cream cheese, softened

¼ cup butter or margarine, softened

2 to 3 teaspoons milk

1 teaspoon vanilla

4 cups powdered sugar

½ cup chopped walnuts, if desired

1 Heat oven to 350°F. Spray 15×10-inch pan with cooking spray. In large bowl, beat eggs, granulated sugar, oil and pumpkin with wire whisk until smooth. Stir in flour, baking powder, baking soda, salt, cinnamon, ginger and cloves. Stir in raisins. In pan, spread batter evenly.

2 Bake 25 to 30 minutes or until toothpick inserted in center comes out clean and bars spring back when touched lightly in center. Cool completely, about 2 hours.

3 In medium bowl, beat cream cheese, butter, milk and vanilla with electric mixer on low speed until smooth. Gradually beat in powdered sugar, 1 cup at a time, on low speed until smooth and spreadable. Spread frosting evenly over bars. Sprinkle with walnuts. For bars, cut into 7 rows by 7 rows. Store covered in refrigerator.

1 Bar: Calories 160 (Calories from Fat 70); Total Fat 8g (Saturated Fat 3g); Cholesterol 25mg; Sodium 95mg; Total Carbohydrate 23g (Dietary Fiber 0g); Protein 1g

In a pinch, use 2½ teaspoons pumpkin pie spice instead of the cinnamon, ginger and cloves.

Snowy Shovels

Prep Time: 55 min ▪ Start to Finish: 55 min ▪ 20 Cookies

½ cup packed brown sugar
½ cup butter or margarine, softened
2 tablespoons water
1 teaspoon vanilla
1½ cups all-purpose flour
⅛ teaspoon salt
10 pretzel rods (about 8½ inches long), cut crosswise in half
⅔ cup white vanilla baking chips
2 teaspoons shortening
Miniature marshmallows (about 80 to 100)
White decorator sugar crystals

1 Heat oven to 350°F. In medium bowl, beat brown sugar, butter, water and vanilla with electric mixer on medium speed, or mix with spoon. Stir in flour and salt. Shape dough into twenty 1¼-inch balls.

2 On ungreased cookie sheet, place pretzel rod halves. Press ball of dough onto cut end of each pretzel rod. Press dough to make indentation to look like shovel, but do not press all the way to the cookie sheet. Bake about 12 minutes or until set but not brown. Cool 2 minutes. Remove from cookie sheet to cooling rack. Cool completely.

3 Cover cookie sheet with waxed paper. Place shovels on waxed paper. In 1-quart saucepan, melt baking chips and shortening over low heat, stirring occasionally, until smooth; remove from heat. Place 4 or 5 marshmallows in bottom portion of shovel to look like pile of snow. Spoon melted white chocolate over marshmallows and bottom portion of shovel; sprinkle with sugar crystals. If desired, drizzle white chocolate over shovel handle. Let stand until chocolate is firm.

1 Cookie: Calories 190 (Calories from Fat 70); Total Fat 8g (Saturated Fat 5g); Cholesterol 15mg; Sodium 180mg; Total Carbohydrate 27g (Dietary Fiber 0g); Protein 2g

Plan ahead! Cookie dough can be covered and refrigerated up to 24 hours before baking. If it's too firm, let stand at room temperature 30 minutes.

Snow-Capped Gingersnaps

Prep Time: 1 hr ■ Start to Finish: 2 hr 30 min ■ About 4 dozen cookies

1 cup packed brown sugar	½ teaspoon ground cloves
¾ cup shortening	¼ teaspoon salt
¼ cup molasses	Granulated sugar
1 egg	1 cup white vanilla baking chips (6 oz)
2¼ cups all-purpose flour	1 tablespoon shortening
2 teaspoons baking soda	Chopped crystallized ginger,
1 teaspoon ground ginger	if desired
1 teaspoon ground cinnamon	

1 In large bowl, mix brown sugar, ¾ cup shortening, the molasses and egg. Stir in flour, baking soda, ground ginger, cinnamon, cloves and salt. Cover; refrigerate at least 1 hour.

2 Heat oven to 375°F. Lightly grease cookie sheet with shortening or cooking spray. Shape dough by rounded teaspoonfuls into balls; dip tops into granulated sugar. On cookie sheet, place balls, sugared sides up, about 3 inches apart.

3 Bake 9 to 12 minutes or just until set. Remove from cookie sheet to cooling rack. Cool completely, about 30 minutes.

4 Cover cookie sheet with waxed paper. In small microwavable bowl, microwave baking chips and 1 tablespoon shortening uncovered on Medium-High 1 minute 30 seconds to 2 minutes, stirring every 15 seconds, until smooth. Dip half of each cookie into melted mixture; sprinkle with crystallized ginger. Place on waxed paper; let stand until coating is firm.

1 Cookie: Calories 100 (Calories from Fat 40); Total Fat 5g (Saturated Fat 2g); Cholesterol 0mg; Sodium 75mg; Total Carbohydrate 13g (Dietary Fiber 0g); Protein 1g

Before measuring molasses, spray the measuring cup with cooking spray; the molasses will come out of the cup much easier.

Gingerbread Cutouts

Prep Time: 1 hr 30 min ▮ Start to Finish: 2 hr 30 min ▮ 10 Dozen cookies

1½ cups granulated sugar	1½ teaspoons ground ginger
1 cup butter or margarine, softened	½ teaspoon salt
3 tablespoons molasses	½ teaspoon ground cardamom
1 egg	½ teaspoon ground cloves
2 tablespoons water or milk	Currants or assorted candies,
3¼ cups all-purpose flour	if desired
2 teaspoons baking soda	Colored sugar or additional sugar,
2 teaspoons ground cinnamon	if desired

1 In large bowl, beat granulated sugar, butter and molasses with electric mixer on medium speed, or mix with spoon, until well mixed. Beat in egg and water until blended. Stir in flour, baking soda, cinnamon, ginger, salt, cardamom and cloves. Cover and refrigerate about 1 hour or until firm.

2 Heat oven to 350°F. On floured surface, roll ⅓ of dough at a time to ⅛-inch thickness. (Keep remaining dough refrigerated until ready to roll.) Cut with floured 2½-inch gingerbread boy or girl cookie cutters. On ungreased cookie sheet, place shapes about 1 inch apart. Decorate with currants or candies. Sprinkle with colored sugar.

3 Bake 6 to 7 minutes or until set. Remove from cookie sheet to cooling rack; cool completely.

1 Cookie: Calories 40 (Calories from Fat 20); Total Fat 2g (Saturated Fat 1g); Cholesterol 5mg; Sodium 40mg; Total Carbohydrate 6g (Dietary Fiber 0g); Protein 0g

"Stitch" the edges of these charming cookies with white candy sprinkles found where cake and cookie decorating supplies are sold.

Gingerbread
Cutouts

Espresso Thumbprint
Cookies, page 102

Espresso Thumbprint Cookies

Prep Time: 45 min ▮ Start to Finish: 1 hr 15 min ▮ About 3½ dozen cookies

Cookies
¾ cup sugar
¾ cup butter or margarine, softened
½ teaspoon vanilla
1 egg
1¾ cups all-purpose flour
3 tablespoons unsweetened baking
    cocoa
¼ teaspoon salt
Crushed hard peppermint candies
    or candy sprinkles, if desired

Espresso Filling
¼ cup whipping cream
2 teaspoons instant espresso coffee
    granules
1 cup milk chocolate chips
1 tablespoon coffee-flavored liqueur,
    if desired

1 Heat oven to 350°F. In large bowl, beat sugar, butter, vanilla and egg with electric mixer on medium speed, or mix with spoon, until well blended. Stir in flour, cocoa and salt until dough forms.

2 Shape dough by rounded teaspoonfuls into 1-inch balls. On ungreased cookie sheets, place balls about 2 inches apart. Press thumb or end of wooden spoon into center of each cookie, but do not press all the way to the cookie sheet.

3 Bake 7 to 11 minutes or until edges are firm. If necessary, quickly remake indentations with end of wooden spoon. Immediately remove from cookie sheets to cooling racks. Cool completely, about 30 minutes.

4 Meanwhile, in 1-quart saucepan, mix whipping cream and instant coffee. Heat over medium heat, stirring occasionally, until steaming and coffee is dissolved. Remove from heat; stir in chocolate chips until melted. Stir in liqueur. Cool about 10 minutes or until thickened.

5 Spoon rounded ½ teaspoon espresso filling into indentation in each cookie. Top with candy sprinkles.

1 Cookie: Calories 90 (Calories from Fat 45); Total Fat 5g (Saturated Fat 3g); Cholesterol 15mg; Sodium 40mg; Total Carbohydrate 10g (Dietary Fiber 0g); Protein 1g

Photo, page 101.

Holiday Melting Moments

Prep Time: 1 hr 15 min ▌ Start to Finish: 2 hr 45 min ▌ About 3½ dozen cookies

Cookies

1 cup butter, softened (do not use margarine)
1 egg yolk
1 cup plus 2 tablespoons all-purpose flour
½ cup cornstarch
½ cup powdered sugar
2 tablespoons unsweetened baking cocoa
⅛ teaspoon salt

Vanilla Frosting

1 cup powdered sugar
2 tablespoons butter or margarine, softened
1 teaspoon vanilla
2 to 3 teaspoons milk
2 candy canes, about 6 inches long, finely crushed

1 In large bowl, beat 1 cup butter and egg yolk with electric mixer on medium speed, or mix with spoon. Stir in flour, cornstarch, ½ cup powdered sugar, the cocoa and salt. Cover; refrigerate about 1 hour or until firm.

2 Heat oven to 375°F. Shape dough by rounded teaspoonfuls into 1-inch balls. On ungreased cookie sheet, place balls about 2 inches apart.

3 Bake 10 to 12 minutes or until set but not brown. Remove from cookie sheet to cooling rack. Cool completely, about 30 minutes.

4 In small bowl, mix all frosting ingredients except candy canes with spoon until smooth and spreadable. Spread frosting evenly on cookies; sprinkle with crushed candy canes.

1 Cookie: Calories 80 (Calories from Fat 45); Total Fat 5g (Saturated Fat 3g); Cholesterol 20mg; Sodium 40mg; Total Carbohydrate 9g (Dietary Fiber 0g); Protein 0g

Holiday Lime Cooler Cookies

Prep Time: 1 hr 25 min ▪ Start to Finish: 1 hr 55 min ▪ About 6 dozen cookies

Cookies

2 cups butter or margarine,
    softened
1 cup powdered sugar
3½ cups all-purpose flour
½ cup cornstarch
2 tablespoons grated lime peel
1 teaspoon vanilla
Granulated sugar

Lime Glaze and Decoration

1 cup powdered sugar
2 tablespoons Key lime or regular
    lime juice
2 tubes (0.68 oz each) green deco-
    rating gel, if desired

1 Heat oven to 350°F. In large bowl, beat butter and 1 cup powdered sugar with electric mixer on medium speed, or mix with spoon. Stir in flour, cornstarch, lime peel and vanilla until well blended.

2 Shape dough into ¾-inch balls. On ungreased cookie sheet, place balls about 2 inches apart. Press bottom of glass into dough to grease, then dip into granulated sugar; press on dough balls until ¼ inch thick.

3 Bake 9 to 11 minutes or until edges are light golden brown. Remove from cookie sheet to cooling rack. Cool completely, about 30 minutes.

4 In small bowl, stir together 1 cup powdered sugar and the lime juice. Stir in additional juice if necessary. Spread glaze over cookies. Squeeze drops of decorating gel on glazed cookies; drag toothpick through gel for marbled design.

1 Cookie: Calories 90 (Calories from Fat 45); Total Fat 5g (Saturated Fat 3g); Cholesterol 15mg; Sodium 35mg; Total Carbohydrate 9g (Dietary Fiber 0g); Protein 0g

If you like using a cookie press, make lime ribbon cookies. Prepare dough as directed, but do not shape it into balls. Place dough in a cookie press with a ribbon tip, and form long ribbons of dough on ungreased cookie sheet; cut ribbons into 3-inch lengths. Continue as directed for baking.

Russian Tea Cakes

Prep Time: 1 hr 5 min ▌ Start to Finish: 1 hr 35 min ▌ About 4 dozen cookies

1 cup butter or margarine, softened	¼ teaspoon salt
½ cup powdered sugar	¾ cup finely chopped nuts
1 teaspoon vanilla	Additional powdered sugar
2¼ cups all-purpose flour	

1 Heat oven to 400°F. In large bowl, beat butter, ½ cup powdered sugar and the vanilla with electric mixer on medium speed, or mix with spoon. Stir in flour and salt. Stir in nuts.

2 Shape dough by rounded teaspoonfuls into 1-inch balls. On ungreased cookie sheet, place balls about 2 inches apart.

3 Bake 8 to 9 minutes or until set but not brown. In small bowl, place additional powdered sugar. Immediately remove cookies from cookie sheet; roll in powdered sugar. Cool completely on cooling rack, about 30 minutes. Roll in powdered sugar again.

1 Cookie: Calories 80 (Calories from Fat 45); Total Fat 5g (Saturated Fat 2g); Cholesterol 10mg; Sodium 40mg; Total Carbohydrate 8g (Dietary Fiber 0g); Protein 0g

Lemon Tea Cakes: Substitute lemon extract for the vanilla and add 1 teaspoon grated lemon peel with the flour. Crush ½ cup lemon drops in food processor or blender. Stir in ¼ cup of the crushed lemon drops with the flour; reserve remaining candy. Bake as directed. Immediately roll baked cookies in powdered sugar; wait 10 minutes, then roll in reserved crushed lemon drops. Reroll, if desired.

Peppermint Tea Cakes: Crush ¾ cup hard peppermint candies in food processor or blender. Stir in ¼ cup of the crushed candies with the flour; reserve remaining candy. Bake as directed. Immediately roll baked cookies in powdered sugar; wait 10 minutes, then roll in reserved crushed candy. Reroll, if desired.

Peppermint
Tea Cakes

Russian Tea
Cakes

Lemon Tea
Cakes

Spritz

Prep Time: 1 hr 50 min ▮ Start to Finish: 2 hr 20 min ▮ About 5 dozen cookies

1 cup butter or margarine, softened
½ cup sugar
1 egg
2½ cups all-purpose flour
¼ teaspoon salt
¼ teaspoon almond extract or vanilla
Few drops of food color, if desired

1 Heat oven to 400°F. In large bowl, beat butter, sugar and egg with electric mixer on medium speed, or mix with spoon. Stir in remaining ingredients.

2 Place dough in cookie press. On ungreased cookie sheet, form desired shapes.

3 Bake 5 to 8 minutes or until set but not brown. Immediately remove from cookie sheet to cooling rack. Cool completely, about 30 minutes.

1 Cookie: Calories 50 (Calories from Fat 30); Total Fat 3g (Saturated Fat 2g); Cholesterol 10mg; Sodium 30mg; Total Carbohydrate 6g (Dietary Fiber 0g); Protein 0g

Chocolate Spritz: Stir 2 ounces unsweetened baking chocolate, melted and cooled, into butter-sugar mixture. Omit food color.

Rum Butter Spritz: Substitute rum extract for the almond extract. Tint dough with food colors. After baking, spread cooled cookies with Rum Butter Glaze: In 1-quart saucepan, melt ¼ cup butter or margarine; remove from heat. Stir in 1 cup powdered sugar and 1 teaspoon rum extract. Stir in 1 to 2 tablespoons hot water until glaze is spreadable. Tint glaze with food color to match cookies.

Spicy Spritz: Stir in 1 teaspoon ground cinnamon, ½ teaspoon ground nutmeg and ¼ teaspoon ground allspice with the flour.

Hanukkah Honey Cookies

Prep Time: 1 hr ▮ Start to Finish: 1 hr ▮ About 3½ dozen cookies

Cookies

⅓ cup powdered sugar

⅓ cup butter or margarine, softened

⅔ cup honey

1 teaspoon almond extract

1 egg

2¾ cups all-purpose flour

1 teaspoon baking soda

½ teaspoon salt

Easy Almond Glaze

2 cups powdered sugar

¼ teaspoon almond extract

2 to 3 tablespoons water

Decorator's Frosting

1 cup powdered sugar

3 to 5 teaspoons water

Blue food color

1 Heat oven to 375°F. Lightly grease cookie sheet. In large bowl, mix ⅓ cup powdered sugar, the butter, honey, 1 teaspoon almond extract and egg. Stir in flour, baking soda and salt until well blended.

2 On lightly floured, cloth-covered surface, roll dough ⅛ inch thick. Cut with cookie cutters. Place about 1 inch apart on cookie sheet.

3 Bake 7 to 8 minutes or until light brown. Immediately remove from cookie sheet to cooling rack; cool completely, about 15 minutes.

4 For almond glaze, in medium bowl, mix 2 cups powdered sugar, ¼ teaspoon almond extract and 2 tablespoons water until smooth. Stir in remaining 1 tablespoon water, 1 teaspoon at a time, until spreadable.

5 For blue frosting, in another medium bowl, mix 1 cup powdered sugar and enough water to make frosting that can be easily drizzled or used in a decorating bag yet hold its shape. Stir in 3 or 4 drops food color.

6 Spread almond glaze over cookies. Decorate with blue frosting.

1 Cookie: Calories 90 (Calories from Fat 20); Total Fat 2g (Saturated Fat 0g); Cholesterol 5mg; Sodium 75mg; Total Carbohydrate 20g (Dietary Fiber 0g); Protein 1g

Double-Espresso Brownies

Amaretto Brownies

Double–Chocolate Chunk Brownies

Candy Bar Brownies

Cookies 'n Creme Brownies

Peanut Butter Swirl Brownies

Walnut Lover's Brownies

Six-Layer Brownies

Brownie Butterscotch Squares

Triple-Vanilla Brownies

Blond Brownies with Brown Sugar Frosting

White Chocolate Chunk Blonde Brownies

5 brownies

Double-Espresso Brownies

Prep Time: 20 min ■ Start to Finish: 1 hr 45 min ■ 50 Brownies

Brownies

1½ cups all-purpose flour

1½ cups granulated sugar

4 teaspoons unsweetened baking cocoa

3 teaspoons instant espresso coffee granules

½ cup water

¾ cup butter or margarine

¾ teaspoon baking soda

⅓ cup buttermilk

1 egg

Frosting

¼ cup unsweetened baking cocoa

½ cup butter or margarine

⅓ cup buttermilk

4½ cups powdered sugar

1 teaspoon instant espresso coffee granules

1 teaspoon vanilla

1 Heat oven to 375°F. Grease bottom and sides of 15×10-inch pan with shortening or cooking spray. In large bowl, mix flour, granulated sugar, 4 teaspoons cocoa and espresso.

2 In 1-quart saucepan, heat water and ¾ cup butter to boiling. Pour over flour mixture; beat with spoon until smooth. Stir in baking soda, ⅓ cup buttermilk and the egg. In pan, spread batter evenly.

3 Bake 18 to 23 minutes or until toothpick inserted in center comes out clean. Cool completely, about 1 hour.

4 In 3-quart saucepan, heat ¼ cup cocoa, ½ cup butter and ⅓ cup buttermilk to boiling over medium heat, stirring frequently; remove from heat. Stir in powdered sugar, 1 teaspoon espresso and vanilla with wire whisk until smooth and spreadable. Spread frosting over brownies. For brownies, cut into 10 rows by 5 rows.

1 Brownie: Calories 130 (Calories from Fat 45); Total Fat 5g (Saturated Fat 3g); Cholesterol 15mg; Sodium 55mg; Total Carbohydrate 20g (Dietary Fiber 0g); Protein 0g

Amaretto Brownies

Prep Time: 20 min ▪ Start to Finish: 1 hr 20 min ▪ 32 Brownies

Brownies
⅔ cup slivered almonds, toasted*
8 oz semisweet baking chocolate
⅓ cup butter or margarine
1¼ cups all-purpose flour
1 cup granulated sugar
1 teaspoon baking powder
½ teaspoon salt

2 tablespoons amaretto
2 eggs

Frosting
2 cups powdered sugar
3 tablespoons butter or margarine, softened
1 tablespoon amaretto
1 to 2 tablespoons milk

1 Heat oven to 350°F. Grease bottom only of 13×9-inch pan with shortening or cooking spray. In food processor, place ⅓ cup of the almonds. Cover and process, pulsing on and off, until almonds are ground. Chop remaining almonds; set aside.

2 In 3-quart saucepan, melt chocolate and ⅓ cup butter over low heat, stirring frequently, until smooth; remove from heat. Stir in ground almonds, flour, granulated sugar, baking powder, salt, 2 tablespoons amaretto and the eggs. Spread batter evenly in baking pan.

3 Bake 22 to 27 minutes or until toothpick inserted in center comes out clean. Cool completely.

4 In medium bowl, mix all frosting ingredients until smooth and spreadable. Spread frosting over brownies. Sprinkle with chopped almonds. For brownies, cut into 8 rows by 4 rows.

*To toast almonds, place in shallow pan. Bake at 350°F for about 10 minutes, stirring occasionally, until golden brown.

1 Brownie: Calories 160 (Calories from Fat 60); Total Fat 7g (Saturated Fat 4g); Cholesterol 20mg; Sodium 80mg; Total Carbohydrate 23g (Dietary Fiber 0g); Protein 2g

Cherry-Almond Brownies: Use ¼ teaspoon almond extract and 1 tablespoon maraschino cherry juice mixed with 1 tablespoon water for the 2 tablespoons amaretto in the brownies. Use ⅛ teaspoon almond extract and 1½ teaspoons maraschino cherry juice mixed with 1½ teaspoons water for the 1 tablespoon amaretto in the frosting.

Double–Chocolate Chunk Brownies

Prep Time: 25 min ■ Start to Finish: 2 hr ■ 24 Brownies

Brownies
1 cup butter or margarine
1 cup granulated sugar
1 cup packed brown sugar
2 teaspoons vanilla
4 eggs
1¼ cups all-purpose flour
¾ cup baking cocoa
¼ teaspoon salt
1 cup semisweet chocolate chunks

6 oz white chocolate, chopped, or
1 cup white vanilla baking chips

Frosting
1½ cups powdered sugar
¼ cup baking cocoa
¼ cup butter or margarine, softened
2 to 3 tablespoons milk
3 oz white chocolate, chopped, or
½ cup white vanilla baking chips
1 teaspoon vegetable oil

1 Heat oven to 350°F. Grease bottom and sides of 13×9-inch pan with shortening or spray with cooking spray. In 4-quart saucepan, melt 1 cup butter over medium heat; remove from heat. Mix in granulated and brown sugar, vanilla and eggs until well blended. Stir in flour, ¾ cup cocoa and salt until well blended. Stir in 1 cup each semisweet and white chocolate chunks. Spread in pan.

2 Bake 30 to 35 minutes or until set. Cool completely, about 1 hour.

3 In large bowl, beat powdered sugar, ¼ cup cocoa, ¼ cup butter and enough of the milk with electric mixer on low speed until frosting is smooth and spreadable. Spread over brownies.

4 In microwavable container, microwave ½ cup white chocolate chunks and the oil uncovered on High 30 to 60 seconds, stirring once or twice, until thin enough to drizzle. When cool enough to handle, place in small resealable food-storage plastic bag; cut off tiny corner of bag. Squeeze bag to drizzle chocolate over frosting. For brownies, cut into 6 rows by 4 rows.

1 Brownie: Calories 360 (Calories from Fat 170); Total Fat 19g (Saturated Fat 10g); Cholesterol 60mg; Sodium 120mg; Total Carbohydrate 46g (Dietary Fiber 2g); Protein 4g

For the best results, use chocolate chunks, not chocolate chips. The chunks contribute to the fudgy texture and richness of the brownies.

Candy Bar Brownies

Prep Time: 40 min ▪ Start to Finish: 2 hr 45 min ▪ 48 Brownies

Brownies

¾ cup butter or margarine, softened

2 tablespoons water

⅔ cup sugar

1 cup semisweet chocolate chips

1 teaspoon vanilla

2 eggs

1 cup all-purpose flour

½ teaspoon baking powder

Candy Bar Topping

1 cup sugar

¼ cup butter or margarine

¼ cup milk

1 cup marshmallow creme

½ cup creamy peanut butter

½ teaspoon vanilla

1½ cups dry-roasted peanuts

40 caramels, unwrapped

¼ cup water

1 cup semisweet chocolate chips

¼ cup butterscotch chips

1 Heat oven to 350°F. Line bottom and sides of 13×9-inch pan with foil, leaving 1 inch of foil overhanging at 2 opposite sides of pan; spray foil with cooking spray.

2 In large microwavable bowl, microwave ¾ cup butter, 2 tablespoons water and ⅔ cup sugar uncovered on High about 1 minute or until mixture just starts to boil; stir until blended. Stir in 1 cup chocolate chips until melted. Stir in 1 teaspoon vanilla and the eggs until well mixed. Stir in flour and baking powder. In pan, spread batter evenly.

3 Bake 18 to 23 minutes or until toothpick inserted in center comes out clean (do not overbake). Cool completely in pan on wire rack, about 30 minutes.

4 In 2-quart saucepan, heat 1 cup sugar, ¼ cup butter and the milk to boiling over medium heat, stirring constantly. Boil 5 minutes, stirring constantly. Stir in marshmallow creme, ¼ cup of the peanut butter and ½ teaspoon vanilla. Pour over brownies. Sprinkle peanuts over top.

5 In 1-quart saucepan, heat caramels and ¼ cup water over medium-low heat, stirring constantly, until caramels are melted; pour over peanuts.

6 In medium microwavable bowl, microwave 1 cup chocolate chips and the butterscotch chips uncovered on High about 1 minute or until softened;

stir until smooth. Stir in remaining ¼ cup peanut butter; spread over caramel layer. Refrigerate at least 1 hour before cutting. Use foil to lift brownies from pan before cutting. For brownies, cut into 8 rows by 6 rows. Store in refrigerator.

1 Brownie: Calories 200 (Calories from Fat 90); Total Fat 11g (Saturated Fat 5g); Cholesterol 20mg; Sodium 105mg; Total Carbohydrate 23g (Dietary Fiber 1g); Protein 3g

Serve these bars in foil liners for a fancier look.

Cookies 'n Creme Brownies

Prep Time: 25 min ▪ Start to Finish: 2 hr 25 min ▪ 20 brownies

1 box (1 lb 2.3 oz) fudge brownie mix
¼ cup water
⅔ cup vegetable oil
2 eggs
1 cup coarsely chopped creme-filled chocolate
    sandwich cookies (about 7 cookies)
½ cup powdered sugar
2 to 4 teaspoons milk

1 Heat oven to 350°F. Grease bottom only of 13×9-inch pan with shortening or spray bottom with cooking spray. In large bowl, stir brownie mix, water, oil and eggs until well blended. In pan, spread batter evenly. Sprinkle cookies over batter.

2 Bake 24 to 26 minutes or until toothpick inserted 2 inches from side of pan comes out almost clean. Cool completely, about 1 hour 30 minutes.

3 In small bowl, stir together powdered sugar and milk until smooth and thin enough to drizzle. Drizzle over brownies. For brownies, cut into 5 rows by 4 rows. Store covered at room temperature.

1 Brownie: Calories 340 (Calories from Fat 160); Total Fat 18g (Saturated Fat 5g); Cholesterol 45mg; Sodium 40mg; Total Carbohydrate 41g (Dietary Fiber 2g); Protein 4g

Change 'em up! With the variety of cookies available, you can easily substitute mint-flavored chocolate sandwich cookies, peanut butter chocolate sandwich cookies or double chocolate cookies to suit your taste.

Peanut Butter Swirl Brownies

Prep Time: 15 min ▪ Start to Finish: 1 hr 50 min ▪ 16 Brownies

⅔ cup granulated sugar
½ cup packed brown sugar
½ cup butter or margarine, softened
2 tablespoons milk
2 eggs
¾ cup all-purpose flour
½ teaspoon baking powder
¼ teaspoon salt
¼ cup peanut butter
⅓ cup peanut butter chips
⅓ cup baking cocoa
⅓ cup semisweet chocolate chips

1 Heat oven to 350°F. Grease 9×9-inch pan. In medium bowl, mix sugars, butter, milk and eggs. Stir in flour, baking powder and salt.

2 Divide batter in half (about 1 cup plus 2 tablespoons for each half). Stir peanut butter and peanut butter chips into 1 half. Stir cocoa and chocolate chips into remaining half.

3 Spoon chocolate batter into pan in 8 mounds, checkerboard style. Spoon peanut butter batter between mounds of chocolate batter. Gently swirl through batters with knife for marbled design.

4 Bake 30 to 35 minutes or until toothpick inserted in center comes out clean. Cool completely, about 1 hour. For brownies, cut into 4 rows by 4 rows.

1 Brownie: Calories 215 (Calories from Fat 100); Total Fat 11g (Saturated Fat 3g); Cholesterol 25mg; Sodium 160mg; Total Carbohydrate 26g (Dietary Fiber 1g); Protein 4g

No peanut butter chips on hand? Butterscotch chips will work just as well.

Walnut Lover's Brownies

Prep Time: 15 min ■ Start to Finish: 1 hr ■ 32 Brownies

Topping
¾ cup packed brown sugar
¼ cup butter or margarine
2 tablespoons all-purpose flour
1 teaspoon vanilla
1 egg
4 cups chopped walnuts

Brownies
¾ cup butter or margarine
4 oz unsweetened baking chocolate
2 cups granulated sugar
1 cup all-purpose flour
1 teaspoon vanilla
4 eggs

1 Heat oven to 350°F. Grease bottom and sides of 13×9-inch pan with shortening or cooking spray. In 2-quart saucepan, heat brown sugar and ¼ cup butter over low heat, stirring occasionally, until butter is melted. Cool slightly. Stir in 2 tablespoons flour, 1 teaspoon vanilla and 1 egg until blended. Stir in walnuts; set aside.

2 In 3-quart saucepan, melt ¾ cup butter and the chocolate over low heat, stirring constantly. Cool slightly. Stir in granulated sugar, 1 cup flour, 1 teaspoon vanilla and 4 eggs. In baking pan, spread batter evenly. Spoon topping evenly over batter.

3 Bake 45 minutes (do not overbake). Cool completely in pan on wire rack. For brownies, cut into 8 rows by 4 rows.

1 Brownie: Calories 280 (Calories from Fat 160); Total Fat 18g (Saturated Fat 6g); Cholesterol 50mg; Sodium 55mg; Total Carbohydrate 24g (Dietary Fiber 1g); Protein 4g

Six-Layer Brownies

Prep Time: 20 min ∎ Start to Finish: 3 hr 15 min ∎ 36 Bars

1 box (1 lb 6.5 oz) supreme brownie mix with pouch of chocolate syrup
⅓ cup butter or margarine, melted
1 egg
1 cup coconut
1 cup toffee bits
1 cup semisweet chocolate chips
1 cup chopped pecans
1 can (14 oz) sweetened condensed milk (not evaporated)

1 Heat oven to 350°F. Grease bottom only of 13×9-inch pan with cooking spray or shortening. (For easier cutting, line pan with foil, then grease foil on bottom only of pan.)

2 In large bowl, stir brownie mix, pouch of chocolate syrup, butter and egg until well blended. Press batter evenly into pan. Bake 10 minutes.

3 Top with coconut, toffee bits, chocolate chips and pecans. Drizzle evenly with condensed milk. Bake 40 to 45 minutes longer or until edges are bubbly and center is set. Cool completely, about 2 hours. For brownies, cut into 9 rows by 4 rows.

1 Brownie: Calories 220 (Calories from Fat 90); Total Fat 10g (Saturated Fat 5g); Cholesterol 45mg; Sodium 90mg; Total Carbohydrate 29g (Dietary Fiber 1g); Protein 2g

Brownie Butterscotch Squares

Prep Time: 10 min ▪ Start to Finish: 3 hr 40 min ▪ 32 Squares

1 box (1 lb 6.5 oz) supreme brownie mix with pouch of chocolate syrup
⅓ cup vegetable oil
¼ cup water
2 or 3 eggs
⅔ cup sugar
⅔ cup light corn syrup
1 cup butterscotch chips
½ cup peanut butter
2 cups corn flakes cereal

1 Heat oven to 350°F. Bake brownie mix for either fudgelike or cakelike brownies, using oil, water and eggs, as directed on box for 13×9-inch pan. Cool completely, about 2 hours.

2 In 2-quart saucepan, heat sugar and corn syrup to boiling, stirring constantly; remove from heat. Stir in butterscotch chips and peanut butter until melted. Stir in cereal. Immediately spread over cooled brownies.

3 Let stand until topping is cool, about 1 hour. For squares, cut into 8 rows by 4 rows. Store tightly covered.

1 Square: Calories 200 (Calories from Fat 60); Total Fat 7g (Saturated Fat 3g); Cholesterol 15mg; Sodium 115mg; Total Carbohydrate 33g (Dietary Fiber 0g); Protein 2g

Expect oohs and aahs when serving these butterscotch- and peanut butter–topped brownies. Pack a plastic knife (rather than a sharp knife) to easily cut brownies.

Triple-Vanilla Brownies

Prep time: 30 minutes ■ Start to Finish: 1 hr 35 minutes ■ 32 Brownies

Brownies

½ cup butter or margarine

1 bag (10 oz) white vanilla baking
    chips (1⅔cups)

1¼ cups all-purpose flour

¾ cup granulated sugar

½ cup chopped nuts

1 teaspoon vanilla

¼ teaspoon salt

3 eggs

Glaze

1½ cups powdered sugar

2 to 3 tablespoons butter or
    margarine, softened

½ to 1 teaspoon vanilla

1 to 2 tablespoons warm water
    or milk

1 Heat oven to 350°F. Grease and flour 13×9-inch pan. In 2-quart saucepan, heat butter and baking chips over low heat, stirring frequently, just until melted. (Mixture may appear curdled.) Remove from heat; cool.

2 Stir in remaining brownie ingredients until well blended. Spread batter evenly in baking pan.

3 Bake 30 to 35 minutes or until toothpick inserted in center comes out clean. Cool completely.

4 In medium bowl, mix all glaze ingredients until smooth and spreadable. Spread glaze over brownies. For brownies, cut into 8 rows by 4 rows.

1 Brownie: Calories 160 (Calories from Fat 70); Total Fat 8g (Saturated Fat 3g); Cholesterol 20mg; Sodium 80mg; Total Carbohydrate 20g (Dietary Fiber 0g); Protein 2g

Blond Brownies with Brown Sugar Frosting

Prep Time: 20 min ∎ Start to Finish: 1 hr 30 min ∎ 36 Brownies

Brownies

1 cup granulated sugar
½ cup packed brown sugar
½ cup butter (do not use
    margarine), softened
1 teaspoon vanilla
2 eggs
1½ cups all-purpose flour
1 teaspoon baking powder
½ teaspoon salt

Brown Sugar Frosting

⅓ cup butter (do not use margarine)
⅔ cup packed brown sugar
3 tablespoons milk
2 cups powdered sugar
½ teaspoon vanilla
½ cup chopped pecans

1 Heat oven to 350°F. In large bowl, beat granulated sugar, ½ cup brown sugar, ½ cup butter, 1 teaspoon vanilla and the eggs with electric mixer on medium speed, or mix with spoon, until light and fluffy. Stir in flour, baking powder and salt. In ungreased 13×9-inch pan, spread batter evenly.

2 Bake 20 to 23 minutes or until golden brown and toothpick inserted in center comes out clean. Cool completely, about 45 minutes.

3 In 2-quart saucepan, melt ⅓ cup butter over low heat. Stir in ⅔ cup brown sugar; cook over low heat 2 minutes, stirring constantly. Stir in milk; cook until mixture comes to a rolling boil. Remove from heat. Gradually stir in powdered sugar and ½ teaspoon vanilla, mixing well with spoon after each addition, until smooth and spreadable. If necessary, add more milk, a few drops at a time. Spread frosting over brownies. Immediately sprinkle with pecans. For brownies, cut into 6 rows by 6 rows.

1 Brownie: Calories 150 (Calories from Fat 50); Total Fat 6g (Saturated Fat 3g); Cholesterol 25mg; Sodium 80mg; Total Carbohydrate 23g (Dietary Fiber 0g); Protein 1g

White Chocolate Chunk Blonde Brownies

Prep Time: 20 min ■ Start to Finish: 2 hr 55 min ■ 36 Brownies

2 cups packed brown sugar
½ cup butter or margarine, softened
2 teaspoons vanilla
½ teaspoon rum extract
2 eggs
2 cups all-purpose flour
1 teaspoon baking powder

¼ teaspoon salt
12 oz white chocolate, chopped, or
    1 bag (12 oz) white vanilla baking
    chips (2 cups)
1 cup chopped walnuts
¼ cup semisweet chocolate chunks
1 teaspoon vegetable oil

1 Heat oven to 350°F. In large bowl, beat brown sugar, butter, vanilla, rum extract and eggs with electric mixer on medium speed until light and fluffy.

2 Beat in flour, baking powder and salt on low speed until well blended. Stir in white chocolate chunks and walnuts. In ungreased 13×9-inch pan, spread batter evenly.

3 Bake 25 to 35 minutes or until top is golden brown and set. Cool completely, about 2 hours.

4 In small microwavable bowl, microwave semisweet chocolate chunks and oil uncovered on High 30 to 60 seconds, stirring every 15 seconds, until melted; stir well. Spread glaze evenly over brownies. If desired, place glaze in small resealable food-storage plastic bag and cut off tiny corner of bag. Squeeze bag to drizzle glaze in diagonal lines over brownies. Let stand until glaze is set. For brownies, cut into 6 rows by 6 rows.

1 Brownie: Calories 180 (Calories from Fat 80); Total Fat 9g (Saturated Fat 4g); Cholesterol 20mg; Sodium 65mg; Total Carbohydrate 24g (Dietary Fiber 0g); Protein 2g

Nuts or not? You could use pecans instead of the walnuts, or you can make the brownies without the nuts if you like.

Cranberry-Apricot Bars

Caramel Apple-Nut Bars

Graham and Fruit Bars

Key Lime Bars

Lemon-Raspberry Cream Bars

Macadamia Nut–Piña Colada Bars

Salted Peanut Chews

Saucepan Granola Bars

Toffee-Pecan Bars

Cardamom-Cashew Bars

Triple-Ginger Bars

German Chocolate Bars

Chewy Chocolate-Oat Bars

Confetti Caramel Bars

White Chocolate–Macadamia-Caramel Bars

Tiramisu Bars

Cinnamon Espresso Bars

Heavenly Cappuccino Praline Bars

6
bars

Cranberry-Apricot Bars

Prep Time: 20 min ▮ Start to Finish: 1 hr 40 min ▮ 16 Bars

Crust
1¼ cups all-purpose flour
½ cup butter or margarine, softened
¼ cup sugar

Filling
½ cup chopped dried apricots
½ cup sweetened dried cranberries
¼ cup sugar
1 tablespoon cornstarch
¼ cup honey
3 tablespoons orange juice

1 Heat oven to 350°F. Line 8-inch square pan with foil; spray foil with cooking spray. In large bowl, beat crust ingredients with electric mixer on low speed until mixture looks like coarse crumbs. Press evenly in pan.

2 Bake 28 to 30 minutes or until light golden brown. Meanwhile, in medium bowl, mix filling ingredients.

3 Remove partially baked crust from oven. Reduce oven temperature to 325°F. Spread filling evenly over crust.

4 Bake 8 to 10 minutes longer or until mixture is set and appears glossy. Cool completely, about 45 minutes. For bars, cut into 4 rows by 4 rows.

1 Bar: Calories 160 (Calories from Fat 50); Total Fat 6g (Saturated Fat 4g); Cholesterol 15mg; Sodium 40mg; Total Carbohydrate 24g (Dietary Fiber 0g); Protein 1g

Try sweetened dried cherries instead of the cranberries for a change.

Caramel Apple-Nut Bars

Prep Time: 15 min ▪ Start to Finish: 2 hr 20 min ▪ 36 Bars

2 cups all-purpose flour
2 cups quick-cooking oats
1½ cups packed brown sugar
1 teaspoon baking soda
½ teaspoon salt
1¼ cups butter or margarine, softened
½ cup caramel topping
3 tablespoons all-purpose flour
1 medium apple, peeled, chopped (1 cup)
½ cup coarsely chopped pecans

1 Heat oven to 350°F. Grease bottom and sides of 13×9-inch pan with shortening or cooking spray. In large bowl, beat 2 cups flour, the oats, brown sugar, baking soda, salt and butter with electric mixer on low speed, or mix with spoon, until crumbly. Press about 3 cups of the mixture in pan. Bake 10 minutes.

2 Meanwhile, in small bowl, mix caramel topping and 3 tablespoons flour. Sprinkle apple and pecans over partially baked crust. Drizzle with caramel mixture. Sprinkle with remaining crust mixture.

3 Bake 20 to 25 minutes or until golden brown. Cool completely, about 1 hour 30 minutes. For bars, cut into 6 rows by 6 rows.

1 Bar: Calories 160 (Calories from Fat 70); Total Fat 8g (Saturated Fat 4g); Cholesterol 15mg; Sodium 130mg; Total Carbohydrate 21g (Dietary Fiber 0g); Protein 2g

Graham and Fruit Bars

Prep Time: 15 min ▪ Start to Finish: 55 min ▪ 24 Bars

⅔ cup all-purpose flour
2 cups honey graham cereal squares, crushed (1 cup)
½ cup packed brown sugar
½ teaspoon ground cinnamon
⅓ cup butter or margarine, melted
⅔ cup apricot jam or preserves

1 Heat oven to 350°F. In medium bowl, mix flour, cereal, brown sugar and cinnamon. Stir in butter until well blended. Reserve ¾ cup of the cereal mixture. Press remaining cereal mixture in bottom of ungreased 8×8-inch pan.

2 Spread jam evenly over cereal mixture. Sprinkle with reserved cereal mixture.

3 Bake 23 to 25 minutes or until top is light golden brown and jam is bubbling. Cool 15 minutes before cutting. For bars, cut into 6 rows by 4 rows.

1 Bar: Calories 95 (Calories from Fat 25); Total Fat 3g (Saturated Fat 2g); Cholesterol 5mg; Sodium 50mg; Total Carbohydrate 16g (Dietary Fiber 0g); Protein 1g

So many spices: For a different flavor, try ¼ teaspoon ground nutmeg in place of the ½ teaspoon cinnamon.

Key Lime Bars

Prep Time: 15 min ▪ Start to Finish: 4 hr 20 min ▪ 36 Bars

1½ cups graham cracker crumbs (24 squares)
⅓ cup butter or margarine, melted
3 tablespoons sugar
1 package (8 oz) cream cheese, softened
1 can (14 oz) sweetened condensed milk (not evaporated)
¼ cup Key lime juice or regular lime juice
1 tablespoon grated lime peel
Additional lime peel, if desired

1 Heat oven to 350°F. Grease bottom and sides of 9×9-inch pan with shortening.

2 In medium bowl, mix cracker crumbs, butter and sugar thoroughly with fork. Press evenly in bottom of pan. Refrigerate while preparing cream cheese mixture.

3 In small bowl, beat cream cheese with electric mixer on medium speed until light and fluffy. Gradually beat in condensed milk until smooth. Beat in lime juice and lime peel. Spread evenly over layer in pan.

4 Bake about 35 minutes or until center is set. Cool 30 minutes. Cover loosely and refrigerate at least 3 hours until chilled. For bars, cut into 6 rows by 6 rows. Garnish with additional lime peel. Store covered in refrigerator.

1 Bar: Calories 110 (Calories from Fat 55); Total Fat 6g (Saturated Fat 3g); Cholesterol 15mg; Sodium 70mg; Total Carbohydrate 12g (Dietary Fiber 0g); Protein 2g

Lemon-Raspberry Cream Bars

Prep Time: 15 min ▪ Start to Finish: 2 hr 10 min ▪ 48 Bars

1 box (1 lb 2.25 oz) lemon cake mix with pudding in the mix
½ cup butter or margarine, softened
2 eggs
¾ cup raspberry preserves
1 package (8 oz) cream cheese, softened
2 tablespoons milk
12 oz white chocolate baking bars, chopped
2 to 3 teaspoons powdered sugar

1 Heat oven 350°F. Grease bottom only of 15×10-inch pan with shortening.

2 In large bowl, mix cake mix, butter and eggs with spoon until well blended. Press evenly in pan with greased or floured fingers.

3 Bake 15 to 20 minutes or until edges are golden brown and crust begins to pull away from sides of pan or toothpick inserted in center comes out clean. Cool 5 minutes. Spread evenly with preserves. Cool 30 minutes.

4 In medium bowl, beat cream cheese and milk with electric mixer on medium speed until smooth; set aside. In 1-quart saucepan, melt white chocolate over low heat, stirring frequently. Add warm melted white chocolate to cream cheese mixture; beat on medium speed until creamy (mixture may look slightly curdled). Carefully spread over preserves.

5 Refrigerate about 1 hour or until set. Sprinkle with powdered sugar. For bars, cut into 8 rows by 6 rows. Store covered in refrigerator.

1 Bar: Calories 140 (Calories from Fat 60); Total Fat 7g (Saturated Fat 4g); Cholesterol 20mg; Sodium 115mg; Total Carbohydrate 17g (Dietary Fiber 0g); Protein 2g

Don't be tempted to use reduced-fat cream cheese (Neufchâtel) instead of regular cream cheese. The white chocolate–cream cheese filling may not get firm enough, even when refrigerated.

Macadamia Nut–Piña Colada Bars

Prep Time: 15 min ▪ Start to Finish: 1 hr 55 min ▪ 24 bars

Bars
1 can (8 oz) crushed pineapple
1 cup all-purpose flour
½ cup butter or margarine, softened
3 tablespoons powdered sugar
2 eggs
1 cup granulated sugar
¾ cup chopped macadamia nuts
½ cup flaked coconut

¼ cup all-purpose flour
½ teaspoon baking powder
¼ teaspoon salt
½ teaspoon rum extract

Pineapple Glaze
½ cup powdered sugar
2 to 3 teaspoons reserved pineapple
   juice

1 Heat oven to 350°F. Grease bottom and sides of 8- or 9-inch square pan with shortening. Drain pineapple well, reserving 3 teaspoons juice for glaze. In medium bowl, mix 1 cup flour, the butter and 3 tablespoons powdered sugar with spoon until flour is moistened. Press evenly in pan. Bake 10 minutes.

2 In medium bowl, beat eggs with wire whisk until blended. Stir in pineapple and remaining bar ingredients. Spread over partially baked crust.

3 Bake 25 to 30 minutes or until golden brown. Cool completely, about 1 hour.

4 Mix all glaze ingredients until smooth and thin enough to drizzle. Drizzle glaze over bars. For bars, cut into 6 rows by 4 rows.

1 Bar: Calories 160 (Calories from Fat 70); Total Fat 8g (Saturated Fat 3g); Cholesterol 30mg; Sodium 70mg; Total Carbohydrate 20g (Dietary Fiber 1g); Protein 2g

Salted Peanut Chews

Prep Time: 10 min ▪ Start to Finish: 1 hr ▪ 36 Bars

1 pouch (1 lb 1.5 oz) peanut butter cookie mix
3 tablespoons vegetable oil
1 tablespoon water
1 egg
3 cups miniature marshmallows
⅔ cup light corn syrup
¼ cup butter or margarine
2 teaspoons vanilla
1 bag (10 oz) peanut butter chips
2 cups crisp rice cereal
2 cups salted peanuts

1 Heat oven to 350°F. Spray bottom only of 13×9-inch pan with cooking spray. In large bowl, stir cookie mix, oil, water and egg until soft dough forms. Press dough in bottom of pan, using floured fingers.

2 Bake 12 to 15 minutes or until set. Immediately sprinkle marshmallows over crust; bake 1 to 2 minutes longer or until marshmallows begin to puff.

3 In 4-quart saucepan, cook corn syrup, butter, vanilla and peanut butter chips over low heat, stirring constantly, until chips are melted. Remove from heat; stir in cereal and peanuts. Immediately spoon cereal mixture over marshmallows. Refrigerate until firm, about 30 minutes. For bars, cut into 9 rows by 4 rows.

1 Bar: Calories 220 (Calories from Fat 100); Total Fat 11g (Saturated Fat 3g); Cholesterol 10mg; Sodium 160mg; Total Carbohydrate 25g (Dietary Fiber 1g); Protein 5g

Skip the cooking spray and line the pan with foil for quick cleanup and easy bar removal.

Saucepan Granola Bars

Prep Time: 10 min ▮ Start to Finish: 1 hr 35 min ▮ 48 Bars

½ cup butter or margarine

2½ cups Original Bisquick mix

2 cups granola with fruit

1 cup packed brown sugar

½ cup chopped nuts

1 teaspoon vanilla

2 eggs

1 Heat oven to 375°F. In 3-quart saucepan, melt butter over low heat. Stir in remaining ingredients until blended. In ungreased 13×9-inch pan, spread mixture evenly.

2 Bake 20 to 25 minutes or until deep golden brown. Cool completely, about 1 hour. For bars, cut into 8 rows by 6 rows.

1 Bar: Calories 90 (Calories from Fat 40); Total Fat 5g (Saturated Fat 2g); Cholesterol 15mg; Sodium 110mg; Total Carbohydrate 11g (Dietary Fiber 0g); Protein 1g

Drizzle cooled bars with melted chocolate chips for a pretty and tasty finish.

Toffee-Pecan Bars

Prep Time: 30 min ▮ Start to Finish: 2 hr ▮ 48 Bars

Crust
¾ cup butter or margarine, softened
⅓ cup packed brown sugar
1 egg
2 cups all-purpose flour

Filling
1 cup butter or margarine
¾ cup packed brown sugar
¼ cup light corn syrup
2 cups coarsely chopped pecans
1 cup swirled caramel & milk chocolate
  chips (from 10-oz bag)

1 Heat oven to 375°F. Grease bottom and sides of 15×10-inch pan with shortening or cooking spray (do not use dark pan).

2 In large bowl, beat ¾ cup butter and ⅓ cup brown sugar with electric mixer on medium speed until light and fluffy. Add egg; beat until well blended. On low speed, beat in flour until dough begins to form. Press dough evenly in pan.

3 Bake 12 to 17 minutes or until edges are light golden brown. Meanwhile, in 2-quart saucepan, heat 1 cup butter, ¾ cup brown sugar and the corn syrup to boiling over medium heat, stirring frequently. Boil 2 minutes without stirring.

4 Quickly stir pecans into corn syrup mixture; spread evenly over partially baked crust. Bake 20 to 23 minutes or until filling is golden brown and bubbly.

5 Immediately sprinkle chocolate chips evenly over hot bars. Let stand 5 minutes to soften. With rubber spatula, gently swirl melted chips over bars. Cool completely, about 1 hour. For bars, cut into 24 squares (6 rows by 4 rows), then cut each square in half to make triangles. Store in refrigerator.

1 Bar: Calories 150 (Calories from Fat 100); Total Fat 11g (Saturated Fat 5g); Cholesterol 20mg; Sodium 50mg; Total Carbohydrate 12g (Dietary Fiber 0g); Protein 1g

Craving other flavors? Try using raspberry-flavored chocolate chips instead of the swirled chips. Or try coarsely chopped walnuts instead of the pecans.

Cardamom-Cashew Bars

Prep Time: 20 min ▪ Start to Finish: 1 hr 5 min ▪ 48 Bars

Crust
½ package (8-oz size) reduced-fat
    cream cheese (Neufchâtel)
½ cup powdered sugar
¼ cup packed brown sugar
2 teaspoons vanilla
1 egg yolk
1½ cups all-purpose flour

Filling
1½ cups packed brown sugar
½ cup fat-free cholesterol-free egg
    product or 2 eggs

3 tablespoons all-purpose flour
2 teaspoons vanilla
½ teaspoon ground cardamom or
    cinnamon
¼ teaspoon salt
1½ cups cashews, pieces and halves

Orange Drizzle
¾ cup powdered sugar
1 tablespoon orange juice

1 Heat oven to 350°F. Grease 13×9-inch pan. In medium bowl, beat cream cheese, ½ cup powdered sugar and ¼ cup brown sugar with electric mixer on medium speed until fluffy. Beat in 2 teaspoons vanilla and egg yolk. Gradually stir in 1½ cups flour to make a soft dough. Press dough evenly in pan. Bake 15 to 20 minutes or until very light brown.

2 In medium bowl, beat all filling ingredients except cashews with electric mixer on medium speed about 2 minutes or until thick and colored. Stir in cashews. Spread over baked crust.

3 Bake 19 to 22 minutes or until top is golden brown and bars are set around edges. Cool completely.

4 Mix all drizzle ingredients until smooth and spreadable. Spread evenly over bars. For bars, cut into 8 rows by 6 rows.

1 Bar: Calories 100 (Calories from Fat 25); Total Fat 3g (Saturated Fat 1g); Cholesterol 10mg; Sodium 55mg; Total Carbohydrate 16g (Dietary Fiber 0g); Protein 2g

This is the bar to make when you're entertaining friends who are watching their waistline. These bars are not only low-fat but also rich and delicious tasting.

Triple-Ginger Bars

Prep Time: 20 min ▯ Start to Finish: 2 hr 45 min ▯ 24 Bars

1 box (1 lb 2.25 oz) white cake mix with pudding in the mix
½ cup butter or margarine, melted
2 eggs
¼ cup finely chopped crystallized ginger
1 tablespoon grated gingerroot
1 teaspoon ground ginger
2 tablespoons decorating sugar crystals

1 Heat oven to 350°F. Grease bottom only of 13×9-inch pan with shortening or spray with cooking spray.

2 In large bowl, mix cake mix, butter and eggs with spoon until well blended. Stir in remaining ingredients except sugar. Press dough in pan, using greased fingers. Sprinkle with sugar.

3 Bake 18 to 23 minutes or until edges are very light golden brown. Cool completely, about 2 hours. For bars, cut into 6 rows by 4 rows.

1 Bar: Calories 140 (Calories from Fat 60); Total Fat 6g (Saturated Fat 3g); Cholesterol 30mg; Sodium 180mg; Total Carbohydrate 20g (Dietary Fiber 0g); Protein 1g

When shopping for gingerroot, look for a piece that has smooth, unblemished skin with no signs of mold. You can find crystallized, or candied, ginger packaged in a plastic bag in the specialty produce section or found in glass jars in the spice aisle.

German Chocolate Bars

Prep Time: 15 min ▪ Start to Finish: 3 hr 55 min ▪ 48 Bars

⅔ cup butter or margarine, softened
1 box (1 lb 2.25 oz) German chocolate cake mix with pudding in the mix
1 container coconut pecan creamy ready-to-spread frosting
1 bag (6 oz) semisweet chocolate chips (1 cup)
¼ cup milk

1 Heat oven to 350°F. Lightly grease bottom and sides of 13×9-inch pan with shortening. In medium bowl, cut butter into cake mix (dry) using pastry blender or crisscrossing 2 knives, until crumbly. Press half of the mixture (2½ cups) evenly in bottom of pan. Bake 10 minutes.

2 Carefully spread frosting over baked layer; sprinkle evenly with chocolate chips. Stir milk into remaining cake mixture. Drop by teaspoonfuls onto chocolate chips.

3 Bake 25 to 30 minutes or until cake portion is slightly dry to the touch. Cool completely, about 1 hour. Cover and refrigerate about 2 hours or until firm. Cut into 8 rows by 6 rows. Store covered in refrigerator.

1 Bar: Calories 135 (Calories from Fat 70); Total Fat 8g (Saturated Fat 4g); Cholesterol 15mg; Sodium 100mg; Total Carbohydrate 15g (Dietary Fiber 0g); Protein 1g

Pack 'em for a picnic! These mouthwatering bars are a great change of pace from the standard brownies typically brought on picnics. Take them right in the pan.

Chewy Chocolate-Oat Bars

Prep Time: 20 min ▌ Start to Finish: 2 hr 15 min ▌ 16 Bars

Filling
¾ cup semisweet chocolate chips
⅓ cup (from 14-oz can) fat-free
  sweetened condensed milk
  (not evaporated milk)

Bars
1 cup whole wheat flour
½ cup quick-cooking oats
½ teaspoon baking powder

½ teaspoon baking soda
¼ teaspoon salt
1 egg
¾ cup packed brown sugar
¼ cup canola or vegetable oil
1 teaspoon vanilla
2 tablespoons quick-cooking oats
2 teaspoons butter or margarine,
  softened

1 Heat oven to 350°F. Spray 8- or 9-inch square pan with cooking spray.

2 In 1-quart heavy saucepan, heat filling ingredients over low heat, stirring frequently, until chocolate is melted and mixture is smooth.

3 In large bowl, stir together flour, ½ cup oats, the baking powder, baking soda and salt; set aside. In medium bowl, stir egg, brown sugar, oil and vanilla with fork until smooth; stir into flour mixture until blended. Reserve ½ cup dough in small bowl for topping.

4 Pat remaining dough evenly in pan (if dough is sticky, spray fingers with cooking spray or dust with flour). Spread filling evenly over dough. Add 2 tablespoons oats and the butter to reserved dough. Mix with pastry blender or fork until well mixed. Place small pieces of mixture evenly over filling.

5 Bake 20 to 25 minutes or until top is golden and firm. Cool completely, about 1 hour 30 minutes. For bars, cut into 4 rows by 4 rows.

1 Bar: Calories 180 (Calories from Fat 60); Total Fat 7g (Saturated Fat 2g); Cholesterol 15mg; Sodium 110mg; Total Carbohydrate 27g (Dietary Fiber 1g); Protein 2g

Try using whole grains
in all your baking. Whole wheat
flour can be substituted for up to
half of the all-purpose flour in
most recipes.

Confetti Caramel Bars

Prep Time: 30 min ▮ Start to Finish: 3 hr 30 min ▮ 32 Bars

1 cup packed brown sugar
1 cup butter or margarine, softened
1½ teaspoons vanilla
1 egg
2 cups all-purpose flour
½ cup light corn syrup
2 tablespoons butter or margarine
1 cup butterscotch chips
1½ to 2 cups assorted candies and nuts (such as candy corn, candy-coated
    chocolate candies and salted peanuts)

1 Heat oven to 350°F. In large bowl, beat brown sugar, 1 cup butter, vanilla and egg with electric mixer on medium speed, or mix with spoon. Stir in flour. Press evenly in bottom of ungreased 13×9-inch pan. Bake 20 to 22 minutes or until light brown. Cool 20 minutes.

2 In 1-quart saucepan, heat corn syrup, 2 tablespoons butter and butterscotch chips over medium heat, stirring occasionally, until chips are melted; remove from heat. Cool 10 minutes.

3 Spread butterscotch mixture evenly over crust. Sprinkle with candies and nuts; gently press into butterscotch mixture. Cover and refrigerate at least 2 hours until butterscotch mixture is firm. For bars, cut into 8 rows by 4 rows, or cut into triangle shapes.

1 Bar: Calories 210 (Calories from Fat 90); Total Fat 10g (Saturated Fat 5g); Cholesterol 25mg; Sodium 80mg; Total Carbohydrate 27g (Dietary Fiber 0g); Protein 2g

White Chocolate–Macadamia–Caramel Bars

Prep Time: 15 min ▮ Start to Finish: 2 hr ▮ 48 Bars

1 box (1 lb 2.25 oz) yellow cake mix with pudding in the mix
½ cup vegetable oil
¼ cup water
2 eggs
½ cup butterscotch caramel topping (from 17-oz jar)
1 package (1 lb 2 oz) refrigerated ready to bake white chunk
     macadamia nut cookies (big variety)

1 Heat oven to 350°F. In large bowl, beat cake mix, oil, water and eggs with electric mixer on low speed until smooth. In ungreased 13×9-inch pan, spread batter evenly.

2 Bake 18 to 22 minutes or until top is golden brown.

3 Remove partially baked crust from oven. In 1-cup microwavable measuring cup, microwave caramel topping on High about 15 seconds or until warm and pourable. Lightly drizzle over crust. Crumble cookies over crust.

4 Bake 18 to 23 minutes longer or until golden brown. Cool completely, about 1 hour. For bars, cut into 8 rows by 6 rows.

1 Bar: Calories 130 (Calories from Fat 60); Total Fat 6g (Saturated Fat 2g); Cholesterol 10mg; Sodium 110mg; Total Carbohydrate 17g (Dietary Fiber 0g); Protein 1g

These brownielike bars are perfect for bag lunches or family picnics.

Tiramisu Bars

Prep Time: 20 min ▪ Start to Finish: 2 hr 20 min ▪ 24 Bars

Bars
¾ cup all-purpose flour
½ cup butter or margarine, softened
¼ cup powdered sugar
1 cup granulated sugar
¾ cup whipping cream
¼ cup butter or margarine, melted
3 tablespoons all-purpose flour
1 tablespoon instant coffee granules
    or crystals

½ teaspoon vanilla
2 eggs
3 oz semisweet baking chocolate,
    grated (about 1¼ cups)

Frosting
1 package (3 oz) cream cheese,
    softened
¼ cup whipping cream
Chocolate curls, if desired

1 Heat oven to 350°F. In medium bowl, beat ¾ cup flour, ½ cup softened butter and the powdered sugar with electric mixer on medium speed until soft dough forms. In bottom of ungreased 8-inch square pan, spread dough evenly. Bake 10 minutes.

2 Meanwhile, in medium bowl, beat remaining bar ingredients, except grated chocolate, with wire whisk until smooth.

3 Sprinkle 1 cup of the grated chocolate over the hot baked crust. Pour egg mixture over chocolate.

4 Bake 40 to 45 minutes or until golden brown and set. Cool completely in pan on wire rack, about 1 hour 15 minutes.

5 In medium bowl, beat cream cheese and ¼ cup whipping cream on medium speed about 2 minutes or until fluffy. Spread evenly over cooled bars. Sprinkle with remaining grated chocolate. For bars, cut into 6 rows by 4 rows. Garnish each with chocolate curl. Store covered in refrigerator.

1 Bar: Calories 180 (Calories from Fat 110); Total Fat 12g (Saturated Fat 8g); Cholesterol 50mg; Sodium 60mg; Total Carbohydrate 15g (Dietary Fiber 0g); Protein 2g

Make mini-desserts!
Cut bars into bite-size squares, and serve in small paper candy cups.

Cinnamon Espresso Bars

Prep Time: 15 min ▮ Start to Finish: 1 hr 35 min ▮ 48 Bars

Bars

1 cup packed brown sugar

⅓ cup butter or margarine, softened

1 egg

1½ cups all-purpose flour

1 tablespoon instant espresso powder

1 teaspoon baking powder

½ teaspoon ground cinnamon

¼ teaspoon salt

¼ teaspoon baking soda

½ cup water

Cinnamon Espresso Glaze

1 cup powdered sugar

¼ teaspoon vanilla

⅛ teaspoon ground cinnamon

4 to 5 teaspoons cold espresso coffee or strong coffee

1 Heat oven to 350°F. Grease bottom and sides of 13×9-inch pan with shortening or spray with cooking spray; coat with flour. In large bowl, beat brown sugar, butter and egg with electric mixer on medium speed until blended, or mix with spoon. Stir in remaining bar ingredients. Spread batter evenly in pan.

2 Bake 20 to 22 minutes or until top springs back when touched in center.

3 Meanwhile, in small bowl, mix all glaze ingredients with spoon until smooth and thin enough to drizzle. Drizzle over bars while warm. Cool completely, about 1 hour. For bars, cut into 8 rows by 6 rows.

1 Bar: Calories 50 (Calories from Fat 15); Total Fat 2g (Saturated Fat 1g); Cholesterol 10mg; Sodium 40mg; Total Carbohydrate 10g (Dietary Fiber 0g); Protein 0g

Espresso gives these bars a rich coffee flavor, but if you don't have it on hand, you could use regular instant coffee granules for a milder flavor.

Heavenly Cappuccino Praline Bars

Prep Time: 25 min ▮ Start to Finish: 1 hr 55 min ▮ 32 Bars

Base
1 teaspoon instant espresso powder
2 teaspoons very hot water
½ cup butter or margarine, softened
¾ cup sugar
1¼ cups all-purpose flour
¾ cup almond brickle chips (not
    chocolate covered)

Espresso Filling
⅓ cup butter or margarine, softened
2 cups powdered sugar
1 teaspoon instant espresso powder
1 tablespoon water
1 teaspoon vanilla

1 Heat oven to 325°F. Grease bottom and sides of 13×9-inch pan with shortening or cooking spray; lightly flour. Dissolve 1 teaspoon espresso in 2 teaspoons hot water. In small bowl, beat espresso, ½ cup butter and granulated sugar with electric mixer on medium speed until fluffy. Beat in flour on low speed. Press evenly in pan.

2 Sprinkle ½ cup of the brickle chips evenly over crust; press in slightly. Bake 15 to 17 minutes or until edges are light golden brown.

3 In medium bowl, beat ⅓ cup butter with electric mixer on medium speed until light and fluffy. Gradually beat in powdered sugar. Dissolve 1 teaspoon espresso in 1 tablespoon water. Beat espresso mixture and vanilla into sugar mixture.

4 Pour filling over hot crust; spread evenly. Bake 28 to 33 minutes or until set. Immediately sprinkle with remaining ¼ cup brickle chips. Cool completely. Cut into 8 rows by 4 rows.

1 Bar: Calories 150 (Calories from Fat 55); Total Fat 6g (Saturated Fat 3g); Cholesterol 30mg; Sodium 90mg; Total Carbohydrate 22g (Dietary Fiber 0g); Protein 1g

Helpful Nutrition and Cooking Information

Recommended intake for a daily diet of 2,000 calories as set by the Food and Drug Administration

Total Fat	Less than 65g
Saturated Fat	Less than 20g
Cholesterol	Less than 300mg
Sodium	Less than 2,400mg
Total Carbohydrate	300g
Dietary Fiber	25g

Calculating Nutrition Information

- The first ingredient is used wherever a choice is given (such as ⅓ cup sour cream or plain yogurt).

- The first ingredient amount is used wherever a range is given (such as 2 to 3 teaspoons).

- The first serving number was used wherever a range is given (such as 4 to 6 servings).

- "If desired" ingredients and recipe variations were not included (such as sprinkle with brown sugar, if desired).

- Only the amount of a marinade or frying oil that is absorbed by the food during preparation was calculated.

Ingredients Used in Recipe Testing and Nutrition Calculations

The following ingredients, based on most commonly purchased ingredients, are used unless indicated otherwise:

- Large eggs, 2% milk, 80%-lean ground beef, canned chicken broth and vegetable oil spread containing at least 65% fat when margarine is used.

- Solid vegetable shortening (not butter, margarine or nonstick cooking spray) is used to grease pans.

Equipment Used in Recipe Testing

- Cookware and bakeware without nonstick coatings were used, unless otherwise indicated.

- No dark-colored, black or insulated bakeware was used.

- When a pan is specified, a metal pan was used; a baking dish or pie plate means ovenproof glass was used.

- An electric hand mixer was used for mixing when mixer speeds are specified.

Metric Conversion Guide

VOLUME

U.S. Units	Canadian Metric	Australian Metric
¼ teaspoon	1 mL	1 ml
½ teaspoon	2 mL	2 ml
1 teaspoon	5 mL	5 ml
1 tablespoon	15 mL	20 ml
¼ cup	50 mL	60 ml
⅓ cup	75 mL	80 ml
½ cup	125 mL	125 ml
⅔ cup	150 mL	170 ml
¾ cup	175 mL	190 ml
1 cup	250 mL	250 ml
1 quart	1 liter	1 liter
1½ quarts	1.5 liters	1.5 liters
2 quarts	2 liters	2 liters
2½ quarts	2.5 liters	2.5 liters
3 quarts	3 liters	3 liters
4 quarts	4 liters	4 liters

WEIGHT

U.S. Units	Canadian Metric	Australian Metric
1 ounce	30 grams	30 grams
2 ounces	55 grams	60 grams
3 ounces	85 grams	90 grams
4 ounces (¼ pound)	115 grams	125 grams
8 ounces (½ pound)	225 grams	225 grams
16 ounces (1 pound)	455 grams	500 grams
1 pound	455 grams	½ kilogram

MEASUREMENTS

Inches	Centimeters
1	2.5
2	5.0
3	7.5
4	10.0
5	12.5
6	15.0
7	17.5
8	20.5
9	23.0
10	25.5
11	28.0
12	30.5
13	33.0

TEMPERATURES

Fahrenheit	Celsius
32°	0°
212°	100°
250°	120°
275°	140°
300°	150°
325°	160°
350°	180°
375°	190°
400°	200°
425°	220°
450°	230°
475°	240°
500°	260°

NOTE: The recipes in this cookbook have not been developed or tested using metric measures. When converting recipes to metric, some variations in quality may be noted.

Index

Page numbers in italics refer to photographs.

Whatever's on the menu,
make it easy with *Betty Crocker*

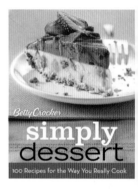

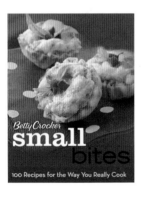